BE LIKE A TREE, PLANTED ...

Prosper in Life!

Kathy

by Minister Kathy McClure

McClure Publishing, Inc.
Oak Lawn, Illinois

ISBN-13 978-0-9790450-0-4
LCCN: 200690923

Cover design by Barron Steward (www.barronsteward.com)
Author photograph by Pete Stenberg
Edited by Marilyn Weishaar for www.theweisrevise.com
Trees by Valerie Gilmer used by permission Copyright © 2006
Arbor Day Tree Chart used by permission of
www.arborday.org

To order additional copies, please contact.
McClure Publishing, Inc.
www.mcclurepublishing.com
800.659.4908
mcclurepublishing@msn.com

Dedication

This book is dedicated to my children and grandchildren. A wise man leaves an inheritance to his children's children. I had already prepared accounts for my children but was still in search for what to leave for my grandchildren. I asked the Lord for his help. While I was writing this book, the Lord told me, "This will be for your children's children."

ACKNOWLEDGMENTS

I thank the following for their contribution to "Be Like A Tree, Planted …"

First and foremost, I praise God and Jesus Christ for causing me to birth this baby ("Be Like A Tree, Planted …").

I call this book, "my SAMUEL."

Thank you:

Dr. Femi for his expertise in editing the manuscript and who also showed me patience is a virtue.

My children for understanding the time I had to spend in the presence of the Lord (my Everything).

My sister Donna for always telling people that she has a sister that is a great woman of God. She sowed good words into my life since we were children.

My bosses for seeing my potential to write the manuscript and for encouraging me to keep my head up. One would always say, "That's impressive."

Kingsley for encouraging me that I can do all things through Christ that strengthens me, and for keeping me laughing during a difficult time in my life. Kingsley went home to be with the Lord in 2006.

Fred for repeatedly assisting me with the table. No matter how many times I asked for help, you were always there.

Valerie for being inspired by Holy Spirit to write a poem about trees.

Lissa Woodson, my publishing consultant, for seeing what God saw in me and helping me open a business and get my book published in less than a month.

(www.macropublishing.com).

Barron Steward (www.barronsteward.com) for designing the book cover and creating my bookmarks, postcards and business cards.

Michael Slaughter (www.2mikeswebdesign.com) for a fabulous website.

Marilyn Weishaar at The Weis Revise (www.theweiserevise.com), for carefully editing the final version of the manuscript.

Pete Stenberg at pdsphoto1@mac.com for taking such a wonderful photo for the book cover and press release, etc. and to Christie Vanderwood for an outstanding job on my makeup.

Last but not least, Walter for making room in my life, so that I could concentrate on bigger and better things. When you are on an assignment, you never know what God will have you do.

BE LIKE A TREE, PLANTED...

*"And he shall be like a tree planted by
the rivers of water, that bringeth forth
his fruit in his season: his leaf also shall
not wither: and whatsoever he doeth shall prosper."*

(Psalm 1:3 KJV)

Foreword

Psalms 1:3 starts with the word "And…" There has to be something before it that goes with it. In Psalms 1:1-2 begins, "*Blessed is the man that walketh not in the counsel of the ungodly, nor standeth in the way of sinners, nor sitteth in the seat of the scornful. But his delight is in the law of the LORD; and in his law doth he meditate day and night.*" Verse one and two speaks of a man blessed, because he decided not to walk with those who walked contrary to the law of the Lord. The Law of the Lord is rules of conduct; particularly rules given by God to Moses by which the Israelites were to live and which were defined in the Pentateuch (the Law of Moses). The Pentateuch consists of the first five books of the Old Testament — Genesis, Exodus, Leviticus, Numbers, and Deuteronomy. The second verse in Psalms shows what happens when a blessed man delights himself in the law of the Lord and meditates on it day and night. Because of the lifestyle of this person, he will be like a tree planted by the rivers of water allowing God to meet all his needs. Thus causing him never to lack and will increase always in substance.

PSALMS 1:3

PSALMS 1:1-2

We must not: 1) walk in the counsel of the ungodly, 2) stand in the way of sinners, and 3) sit in the seat of the scornful. All three are listed under evildoers. The ungodly do not want to have anything to do with the Lord; they rebel against it. Sinners do not fear God or have knowledge of the path that leads to righteousness and holiness of God. The scornful put their mouths against the things of God; they will not adhere to sound wisdom, but run their feet to evil. They boast and show no regret for their sins; in fact they see them as something of which to be proud.

Once we separate ourselves from evildoers, we can delight in the law of the Lord, which is His Word. We must replace the deeds of evildoers with delighting in the Word of God, which is His law. Throughout this book we will see how the Word of God will cause us to delight in the law of the Lord so that we will be like a tree planted by rivers of water. We will see how meditating on His Word will help in times of trouble. We will develop a personal relationship with the Father through His Word and learn how to walk in His Word day and night.

When we see others walking contrary to the Word of God, we should pray for them and never look down on them. There are times we will fall short to God's Word. Remember that a righteous man falls seven times, but the Lord will up hold him in His right hand. We should allow ourselves to be open to make mistakes because in our mistakes we grow if we learn from them.

God created everything to be productive, to produce after its own kind, to multiply. Everything He created was good. He gave man and woman dominion and authority over everything. He created us to subdue the earth.

All creations typify Christ. One in particular was on the third day when God separated the waters above from the waters beneath and the land came up out of the water. In Genesis 2:9 the tree of life is a type of Christ. When Christ was resurrected, He came from the tomb and ascended into Heaven and sits on the right hand of the Father. He took the keys to death, hell and the grave giving us a right to the tree of life.

GENESIS 2:9

Holy Spirit moved upon the earth to create whatever God spoke. After Christ ascended, the Holy Spirit descended upon the earth.

God the Father, God the Word, and God the Holy Spirit are witnesses in Heaven and they are one. Remember the Word was made flesh and dwelt among us, according to John 1:14.

JOHN 1:14

Introduction

"What is a tree."

The main parts of a tree are leaves, which are connected to branches, which are connected to the trunk, which is connected to the roots.

But a tree is much more than that. Many creatures live in trees. People sit under them with a blanket to relax or keep warm in winter or cool in the summer. The wood can be burned for warmth. A tree can provide food such as fruits, nuts, maple syrup, and chocolate.

Trees look different depending on the season: In the winter we see only branches, in the spring we see buds that will turn into flowers, in the summer we see hundreds of leaves, in the fall we see the leaves turn colors and drop to the ground.

Leaves come in different sizes and shapes. Some are narrow and some are wide. Some edges are smooth and some are jagged. Some have shapes that are simple, and some are not. A simple leaf has a single blade. A compound leaf has many smaller leaves that make up the whole. Leaves make food for the tree but to do so they need water, nutrients, and sunlight. Veins help move food and water to the leaf. Trees have branches, which make great places for birds to sit or to build a shelter (nest). Branches are connected to the tree's trunk through which food and water move to the branches and out to the leaves. Bark protects the tree from nature, animals, and people. Some trees have smooth bark while others have rough bark like an alligator's skin. Roots provide the foundation to keep trees from falling over, serve as a storage place for food that moves down through the veins in the leaves to the branches and trunk, and bring water and nutrients to the trunk.

Trees can be tall or short; some are so small they fit in the palm of a hand. Trees come in different shapes — skinny, fat, and sprawling. Trees improve the air by providing oxygen. They give us shade, wood for our houses, toys, paper supplies and more. Trees provide homes — and in some cases food — for birds, bugs, and animals. Caterpillars eat leaves; beavers eat bark.

Trees are a special resource; they need us and we need them. There are numerous ways we can protect this important part of our lives:

- Do not nail signs to a tree.

- Recycle paper; write on both sides of paper, reuse shopping bags and folders.
- Use a rag or a sponge instead of a paper towel if at all possible.
- Protect wood floors, doors and trim with varnish or stain.

For more information on trees, please visit:

www.domtar.com.

Christic Typifies the Tree

Christ was born of a virgin, ministered and taught very powerfully, was beaten to death, buried, and resurrected. What looked like death was not death, it was a metamorphosis. It's like a tree that looks dead when the leaves fall to the ground, but when spring comes the leaves start budding; life is renewed. Christ nurtures us and supplies us with God's Word the same way veins provide food and water to the leaf. Jesus Christ is the Word, which is food for our souls. We can find rest in Jesus Christ. He shelters and protects us from the storms of life. Jesus came that we might have life and have it more abundantly. He came to redeem our relationship with the Father. The best decision we will ever make is to give our lives to Him. Jesus makes our life with the Father more meaningful.

Isaiah 7:14 says, *"Therefore the Lord himself shall give you a sign; Behold, a virgin shall conceive, and bear a son, and shall call his name Immanuel."* God saw Jesus' mother, Mary, diligent in worship. She spent time in the temple, in His presence, so He chose her to conceive the Lamb of God. She was espoused to Joseph and an angel came to him in a dream to tell him that the baby's name would be called

ISAIAH 7:14

Immanuel; "God with us."

LUKE 2:43-52

Luke 2:43-52 describes the boyhood of Jesus. He was not teaching but was listening and asking questions at the age of 12 in the Temple. The quality and depth of His words and understanding of the scriptures astounded the elders. His parents returned from a day's journey from Jerusalem to Galilee and discovered he was not with them. They came back looking for Him to be with relatives and acquaintances. They were really worried about Jesus. Three days later they found Him among the teachers in Jerusalem where He told them He was about His Father's business.

Some believe that His ministry only begun after the forty days of fasting, temptation, and selection of disciples. The nature of His mission and ministry truly began in the temple when he was twelve that was followed by home training under His earthly parents until he was thirty. Three years later He finished His mission on the cross. No man took His life; Jesus gave His life for us. He became an advocate to pray our hearts' desire.

In order to receive the desires of our hearts we must spend time in the presence of the Lord and delight ourselves in Him. God will supply all our needs according to His riches in glory, which is through Christ Jesus. John 14:6 tells us that no man can come to the Father but by Jesus ("*Jesus saith unto him, I am the way, the truth, and the life: no man cometh unto the Father, but by me.*"). And no man can come to Jesus unless God draws him (John 6:44 "*No man can come to me, except the Father which hath sent me draw him: and I will raise him up at the last day.*").

JOHN 6:44

God made us in His own image after His likeness, but He created us in all shapes and sizes. He gave us authority and dominion on this earth. Wherever two or three are gathered in His name there He is in their midst such that whatever they bind on earth will be bound in Heaven and whatever they loose on earth will be loosed in Heaven (first natural then spiritual). We have authority to speak things into existence exactly as our Father, who is in Heaven. We have authority to command and decree things to be so. As long as we are obedient to His Word, we are grounded and rooted on a solid foundation.

The Word contains a parable of two men building houses. One built his house upon a solid foundation while the other built his house upon sand. The one who built upon the sand is likened to one that is disobedient. When the storms came and the winds blew, his house fell. Being obedient keeps us from falling when crises arise.

There will be times in our lives when it seems we will not make it but if we hold onto God's unchanging hands we will be able to stand and nothing will harm us. We must wait on the Lord. He shall renew our strength, according to Isaiah 40:31 *"But they that wait upon the LORD shall renew their strength; they shall mount up with wings as eagles; they shall run, and not be weary; and they shall walk, and not faint."*

A Day For Planting Trees

THERE IS A TIME FOR EVERYTHING UNDER THE SUN ACCORDING TO THE BOOK OF ECCLESIASTES 3:2 "...*A TIME TO PLANT*...")

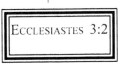

National Arbor Day is the last Friday in April, but many states observe on the day according to their best tree-planting times, listed along with each state's official tree in the following table:

ARBOR DAY DATES ACROSS AMERICA

Alabama Last full week of February (State Tree: Longleaf Pine)	**Alaska** Third Monday in May (State Tree: Sitka Spruce)
Arizona Third Friday in April (State Tree: Paloverde)	**Arkansas** Third Monday in March (State Tree: Pine)
California March 7 - 14 (State Tree: California Redwood)	**Colorado** Third Friday in April (State Tree: Blue Spruce)
Connecticut Last Friday In April (State Tree: White Oak)	**Delaware** Last Friday in April (State Tree: American Holly)
Dist Of Columbia Last Friday in April (State Tree: Scarlet Oak)	**Florida** Third Friday in January (State Tree: Cabbage Palmetto)
Georgia Third Friday in February (State Tree: Live Oak)	**Hawaii** First Friday in November (State Tree: Kukui)

Idaho Last Friday in April (State Tree: Western White Pine)	**Illinois** Last Friday in April (State Tree: White Oak)
Indiana Last Friday in April (State Tree: Tuliptree)	**Iowa** Last Friday in April (State Tree: Oak)
Kansas Last Friday in April (State Tree: Cottonwood)	**Kentucky** First Friday in April (State Tree: Tulip Poplar)
Louisiana Third Friday in January (State Tree: Baldcypress)	**Maine** Third Full Week in May (State Tree: Eastern White Pine)
Maryland First Wednesday in April (State Tree: White Oak)	**Massachusetts** Last Friday in April (State Tree: American Elm)
Michigan Last Friday in April (State Tree: Eastern White Pine)	**Minnesota** Last Friday in April (State Tree: Red Pine)
Mississippi Second Friday in February (State Tree: Southern Magnolia)	**Missouri** First Friday in April (State Tree: Flowering Dogwood)
Montana Last Friday in April (State Tree: Ponderosa Pine)	**Nebraska** Last Friday in April (State Tree: Cottonwood)
Nevada Last Friday in April (State Tree: Singleleaf Pinon and Bristlecone Pine)	**New Hampshire** Last Friday in April (State Tree: Paper Birch)
New Jersey Last Friday in April (State Tree: Northern Red Oak)	**New Mexico** Second Friday in March (State Tree: Pinon)
New York Last Friday in April (State Tree: Sugar Maple)	**North Carolina** First Friday following March 15 (State Tree: Pine)

North Dakota First Friday in May (State Tree: American Elm)	**Ohio** Last Friday in April (State Tree: Ohio Buckeye)
Oklahoma Last Full Week of March (State Tree: Eastern Redbud)	**Oregon** First Full Week of April (State Tree: Douglasfir)
Pennsylvania Last Friday in April (State Tree: Eastern Hemlock)	**Rhode Island** Last Friday in April (State Tree: Red Maple)
South Carolina First Friday in December (State Tree: Cabbage Palmetto)	**South Dakota** Last Friday in April (State Tree: Black Hills spruce)
Tennessee First Friday in March (State Tree: Tulip Poplar)	**Texas** Last Friday in April (State Tree: Pecan)
Utah Last Friday in April (State Tree: Blue Spruce)	**Virginia** Last Friday in April (State Tree: Flowering Dogwood)
Washington Second Wednesday in April (State Tree: Western Hemlock)	**West Virginia** Second Friday in April (State Tree: Sugar Maple)
Wisconsin Last Friday in April (State Tree: Sugar Maple)	**Wyoming** Last Monday in April (State Tree: Cottonwood)

For more information call (888) 448-7337 or visit

www.arborday.org.

On the Third Day

(Genesis 1:9-13)

GENESIS 1:9-13

"And God said, let the waters under the heaven be gathered together unto one place, and let the dry land appear: and it was so. And God called the dry land Earth; and the gathering together of waters called he Seas: and God saw that it was good. And God said, Let the earth bring forth grass, the herb yielding seed, and the fruit tree yielding fruit after his kind, whose seed is in itself, upon the earth: and it was so. And the earth brought forth grass, and herb yielding fruit, whose seed was in itself, after his kind: and God saw that it was good. And the evening and the morning were the third day."

On the third day the land was recovered, life came forth. God separated the waters above from the waters beneath. The waters of death buried Christ. According to scriptures, He was resurrected on the third day. He brought us an inheritance, incorruptible and undefiled, that does not fade away, according to I Peter 1:3-4. He gave us the right to

I PETER 1:3-4

come boldly to the throne of grace to obtain mercy in a time of need. He gave us a place to go to find rest for our souls. He gave us so much.

As He was buried for our sins, we were buried with Him through our sins. Once we accept Christ as our personal savior we, too, will realize we were raised with Him. We were given the same authority, power, and dominion as Christ. Thus circumstances of life that knock us down cannot keep us down. It reminds me of the Weeble, a toy that was popular when I was a little girl. Commercials declared, "Weebles wobble but they do not fall down."

As we go through life, we experience hardships that put us in a state of death. We find ourselves buried under the struggle until we realize we are not designed and created to stay in that state. It is not as bad as it seems. While our problems appear to consume us, God puts us through the process of vegetating to develop undergrowth. As soon as we start sprouting, we come out and move forward and grow. We expand, just like a tree.

Old traditions took us this far but they will not take us farther. It is time for change. Every year we should have more knowledge and understanding than the previous year. We should always be eager to learn and become wiser in order to walk in wisdom. God is looking for a third day church — a church that allows the resurrection of Jesus Christ to come alive. The church is not a brick and mortar building; we are the church. Only through the Spirit of God will we move forward. The wind of the Spirit will carry us into new areas. You have heard the sayings, "It's hard to teach an old dog new tricks," or, "You can take a horse to water, but you cannot make *it* drink *the wate*r." Some people really do not want to change. No one can convince them something new is happening through the Spirit of the Lord. The Bible says He will do a new thing; it shall spring forth.

I was in a ministry that thought if someone did something differently it was not the way of God. They followed the program thought of and written by man to the letter. If the Spirit of the Lord wanted to get in, He had to wait until the leading pastor said it was time. By that time the Spirit was gone.

God has pastors in charge to keep His order in His house, however, if some leaders are not where they belong in God, God will raise another. We should always submit to authority rather than try to override it. We must take whatever ill feelings we may have about the leaders to the Lord. We must also check with our hearts, because if there is anything in us that does not want to submit to authority, we must remove it. We must seek God for instructions and guidance, pray to God to help the ministry and watch Him manifest His heart for the ministry.

A resurrected church will welcome new ideas and new revelation about God. There was a time when we could not wear what we wanted to church. Gospel artists were required to dress up before people would listen to their music. Every 't' had to be crossed and every 'i' dotted which meant we had to look perfect. Nothing could be out of place on the outside. Traditionally if we looked saved, we were. Today, the Spirit of the Lord is manifesting in the heart of man through the layers of clothes. We had to stop looking on the outside and look on the inside of man by checking the person's character. We must pay attention to how people treat others, listen to what they say, and see if their actions line up with their words. Are they walking in integrity? Are they honest with themselves? If they are not honest with themselves, they will not be honest with us. People must be true to themselves before they can be true to anyone else. God requires us to walk in the Spirit of excellence. I want to make this perfectly clear, I have not arrived and am still learning how to reach the mark of the high calling which is by Christ Jesus.

A Third Day Church will teach that a relationship with God is necessary to live a fulfilled life. When we have a personal relationship with the Father, we do things He likes us to do. We realize that the Ark of the Covenant is the actual presence of the Lord.

The Ten Commandments were housed in The Ark of the Covenant, a beautiful chest made of acacia or shittim wood, a cubit and a half wide and high, two cubits long, and completely covered with the purest gold. A rim of gold surrounded the top or lid, the mercy-seat; two gold rings holding two gold-covered poles used to carry the ark adorned either side. Two cherubim over the ark, with their faces turned toward each other graced each end. Their outspread wings over the top of the ark formed the throne of God, while the ark itself was his footstool.

The ark rested in the "Holy of Holies," in such a way that one end of each carrying poles touched the veil, which separated the two sections of the tabernacle. Later it held the book of the Law, manna bread, and Aaron's rod. Deuteronomy 31:26 tells us, *"Take this book of the law, and put it in the side of the ark of the covenant of the LORD your God, that it may be there for a witness against thee."* Exodus 16:33 says, *"And Moses said unto Aaron, Take a pot, and put an omer full of manna therein, and lay it up before the LORD, to be kept for your generations."* Numbers 17:10 tells us, *"And the LORD said unto Moses, Bring Aaron's rod again before the testimony, to be kept for a token against the rebels; and thou shalt quite take away their murmurings from me, that they die not."* The ark was a symbol of God's promise for Israel. It was part of

DEUT. 31:26

EXODUS 16:33

NUMBERS 17:10

their tabernacle, a movable reminder of their exodus and of God's leadership.

The covenant relationship makes us confident in that knowledge that God has already given us His protective care, His assurance, His guidance, and His presence. It also has its requirements — obedience and loyalty to the Father. The Old Covenant given to Abraham was based on grace, law, and obedience and is often referred to as the Old Testament. The new covenant was given to us of grace through God's Son, Jesus Christ. The New Covenant, based on the administration of grace is often called the New Testament.

A Third Day Church will teach their members the events of the Feasts and Festivals celebrated in the Old Testament. These are important events to God, so therefore, they should be important to us.

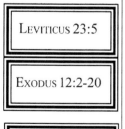

- Passover (Exodus 12:2-20; Leviticus 23:5) Commemorates God's deliverance of Israel out of Egypt.
- Feast of Unleavened Bread (Leviticus 23:6-8) Commemorates God's deliverance of Israel out of Egypt. Includes a Day of First fruits for barley harvest.
- Feast of Weeks or Harvest — Pentecost

— (Exodus 23:16; 34:22; Leviticus 23:15-21)

Commemorates the giving of the law at Mount Sinai. Includes a Day of First fruits for the wheat harvest.

- Feast of Trumpets — Rosh Hashanah — (Leviticus 23:23-25; Numbers 29:1-6) Day of the blowing of the trumpets to signal the beginning of the civil new year.

- Day of Atonement — Yom Kippur — (Leviticus 23:26-33; Exodus 30:10) On this day the high priest makes atonement for the nation's sin. Also a day of fasting.

- Feast of Booths, on Tabernacles — Sukkot — (Leviticus 23:33-43; Numbers 29:12-39; Deuteronomy 16:13) Commemorates the forty years of wilderness wandering.

- Feast of Dedication, or Festival of Lights — Hanukkah — (John 10:22) Commemorates the purification of the temple by Judas Maccabaeus in 164 B.C.

- Feast of Purim, or Esther (Esther 9) Commemorates the deliverance of the

EXODUS 23:16; 34:22 LEVITICUS 23:15-21

LEVITICUS 23:23-25; NUMBERS 29:1-6

LEVITICUS 23:26-33; EXODUS 30:10

LEVITICUS 23:33-43; NUMBERS 29:12-39; DEUTERONOMY 16:13

JOHN 10:22

ESTHER 9

Jewish people in the days of Esther.[1]

The Feast of Tabernacle includes the Day of Atonement. There are seven blessings of the Atonement in the book of Joel:

JOEL 2:23

1. Double Portion (Joel 2:23) *"Be glad then, ye children of Zion, and rejoice in the LORD your God: for he hath given you the former rain moderately, and he will cause to come down for you the rain, the former rain, and the latter rain in the first month."*

JOEL 2:24

2. Financial Promises (Joel 2:24) *"And the floors shall be full of wheat, and the fats shall overflow with wine and oil."*

JOEL 2:25

3. Restoration (Joel 2:25) *"And I will restore to you the years that the locust hath eaten, the cankerworm, and the caterpiller, and the palmerworm, my great army which I sent among you."*

JOEL 2:26

4. Special Miracles (Joel 2:26) *"And ye shall eat in plenty, and be satisfied, and praise the name of the LORD your God, that hath dealt wondrously with you: and my people shall never be ashamed."*

JOEL 2:27

5. Divine Presence (Joel 2:27) *"And ye shall know that I am in the midst of Israel, and that I am the LORD your God, and none else: and my people shall never be*

[1] *Reference taken from page 92 of The Student Bible Dictionary by Karen Dockrey, Johnnie Godwin, and Phyllis Godwin.*

ashamed."

6. Blessings for our sons and daughters (Joel 2:28) "*And it shall come to pass afterward, that I will pour out my spirit upon all flesh; and your sons and your daughters shall prophesy, your old men shall dream dreams, your young men shall see visions:*"

JOEL 2:28

7. Deliverance to him who call on the name of the Lord (Joel 2:32) "*And it shall come to pass, that whosoever shall call on the name of the LORD shall be delivered: for in mount Zion and in Jerusalem shall be deliverance, as the LORD hath said, and in the remnant whom the LORD shall call.*"

JOEL 2:32

In the New Testament in the book of Acts we find something similar to what was said in the book of Joel. Acts 2:17-18 tells us, "*And it shall come to pass in the last days, saith God, I will pour out of my Spirit upon all flesh: and your sons and your daughters shall prophesy, and your young men shall see visions, and your old men shall dream dreams: And on my servants and on my handmaidens I will pour out in those days of my Spirit; and they shall prophesy:*"

ACTS 2:17-18

We cannot study or understand the New Testament without referring to the Old Testament as a foundation upon which to build. The Old Testament consists of the Law, the

History, Poetry, and the Prophets (Major and Minor). The New Testament consists of the Four Gospels, History, the Pauline Epistles, the General Epistles, the Book of Prophecy. The New Testament brings us to the knowledge of Baptism, Communion, and Salvation. Truth unfolds from the Old to the New Testament. Now we are walking in the knowledge of who God is. In the Old Testament animals were sacrificed for sin offerings. In the New Testament Jesus came as the sacrificial Lamb slain for our sins. We have a right to the throne of grace.

Through prayer we may enter behind the veil that was torn in two. The mercy seat is located in the Holy of Holies, the throne of grace. We are able to obtain mercy in a time of trouble. We should stop carrying around our troubles and start carrying the very presence of God. In His presence all our needs are met and there is fullness of joy.

The tabernacle was divided in two portions — the veil. The Holy Place and the Holy of Holies. The Bible states that after Jesus was resurrected the veil was torn in two, the earth quaked and the dead got up and walked. We have a right to enter into the Holy of Holies at the mercy seat. We must begin with praise and thanksgiving. In order to go in farther we must start telling the Lord who He is by calling Him by name. (In chapter four of this book, there are several names of God.) Once we get into the Holy of Holies, we can lift up our concerns to the Lord. This tabernacle is found inside us, in the depths of our souls.

Communion — the Lord's Supper is a form of fellowship with God. When we take Holy Communion, we are doing so in fellowship with Christ and His disciples. We take communion in remembrance of Christ's death. The bread represents Christ's body and the wine represents His blood. Although we eat the bread and drink the wine by mouth, we do it by faith which is the mouth or hand of the soul by the power of the Holy Spirit. This should be done often until the day of Christ's return.

Baptism — means to immerge, submerge in water. Baptism does not save us, but it signifies the death, burial, and resurrection of Jesus Christ. Going under the water is like a dead person being placed in the ground (the old way of life). Rising out of the water is coming up from the old ways and entering into a new life. Baptism is not a requirement for salvation. Those who receive baptism gives witness to the death and resurrection of Christ.

In order to be saved and receive salvation we must confess with our mouths the Lord Jesus and believe in our hearts that God raised Jesus from the dead. Romans 10:9 tell us, *"That if thou shalt confess with thy mouth the Lord Jesus, and shalt believe in thine heart that God hath raised*

ROMANS 10:9

him from the dead, thou shalt be saved." When we confess the Lord Jesus, we do not care who agrees or disagrees. We speak about Jesus as being the Lamb that was slain to redeem us to God. He is the Messiah. We confess that Jesus came to reconcile our relationship back with the Father. When we believe that God raised Jesus from the dead, we walk according to the Word of God.

When Jesus ascended, the Holy Spirit descended upon the earth. Paul asked a question in Acts 19:2, "*He said unto them, Have ye received the Holy Ghost since ye believed? And they said unto him, We have not so much as heard whether there be any Holy Ghost.*" The scripture says Paul laid hands on them; they spoke in tongues and prophesied. We do not have a problem regarding prophecy; the part about speaking in tongues has been controversial to some people for many, many years. Acts 19:6 says, "*And when Paul had laid his hands upon them, the Holy Ghost came on them; and they spake with tongues, and prophesied.*" In my opinion it is according to our faith and what we believe. When we rely on our intellect to comprehend speaking in tongue, we cannot fathom it. It can only be done through the spirit that dwells in us. We can only prophesy according to the measure of our faith. Romans 12:6 tells us, "*Having then gifts differing according to the grace that is given to us, whether prophecy, let us prophesy according to the proportion of faith;*"

ACTS 19:2

ACTS 19:6

ROMANS 12:6

Paul said in Romans 12:1, "*I beseech you therefore, brethren, by the mercies of God, that ye present your bodies a living sacrifice, holy, acceptable unto God, which is your reasonable service.*" Reasonable in this scripture means that is the least we can do.

ROMANS 12:1

A Third Day Church will teach that we are kings. The Bible says that Jesus is King of kings and Lord of lords. Although we live in a democracy society, we are still kings. We are kings and lords. Kings rule and have dominion over territory. Once a king decrees something, the citizens follow what he says. What is a Kingdom? The Kingdom is a state government with all characteristics of a state. Its components are:

- A King
- A Territory
- A Constitution
- A Citizenry
- Law
- Privilege
- A Code of Ethics
- An Army
- A Commonwealth, and
- A Social Culture

Components necessary for a Kingdom to function

effectively include:

- A Health program - Healing
- An Education program - Teaching ministry of the Holy Spirit
- A Taxation system - Tithing
- A Central Communication system - Gifts of the Spirit
- A Diplomatic Corps - Ambassadors of Christ
- A System of Administration - The Ministration of the Spirit through mankind called the Church
- An Economy - a system of Giving and Receiving (seed time and harvest time)[2]

A Third Day Church knows that God is bringing everyone together in one place. Churches around the globe send missionaries to other countries to teach and minister the Word of God and interpret its message.

A Third Day Church will teach it is okay to have and use a professional talent in the workforce and still serve God. Market Place Ministry is done in the work place. We are the caretakers of the earth. We are suppose to rule the earth and have dominion on it.

A Third Day Church realizes that children and the youth ministry are very important to our future. Children have their own way, a more energetic way, of praising God. Once the

[2] *Rediscovery the Kingdom by Myles Munroe*

church begins to understand the difference between adult worship and youth worship, we will be better equipped for the youth ministry. We should teach our youth from generation to generation the laws of God. Recently an elder told me to arrest those spirits that are not like God in my children; command that those spirits lose their hold over my children's minds; bind up the spirit of low self-esteem and loosen the spirit of confidence and encouragement.

A Third Day Church will do things before it is done in the world. God created us to be designer originals not copycats. Corporate businesses are conducting seminars on growing and expanding. The Third Day Church is doing the same for spiritual and natural growth and expansion as it teaches its members to become entrepreneurs.

A Third Day Church recognizes gifts in others and help stir them up to edify the body of Christ. They are not concerned whether we are doing better than they are. They realize the more disciples there are, the better equipped all of us will be. In these last of the last days, we are dealing with evil forces that are stronger than they ever been. It will take an army of Christians to come together and be on one accord to fight and defeat the kingdom of darkness.

A Third Day Church realizes that technology is growing rapidly and is moving with it. Messages can be downloaded on cell phones and computers. Books are in electronic form. Messages are put on CDs and DVDs. God is not wasting time.

Chapter Two
The Tree Of Life

(Genesis 2: 8-9)

In Genesis 2:8-9 we find "...*that the Lord God planted a garden eastward in Eden; and there he put the man whom he had formed. And out of the ground made the Lord God to grow every tree that is pleasant to the sight; and good for food; the tree of life also in the midst of the garden, and the tree of knowledge of good and evil.*"

God formed Adam from the dust of the earth and blew His breath (life) into man and man became a living soul. He put Adam to sleep, performed a spiritual surgery, and created Eve from the seat of Adam's affection — his rib.

Adam and Eve were able to eat from every tree in the garden except the tree of knowledge of good and evil. Eve let the serpent convince her that she would not die; she was thinking naturally. I believe God meant spiritually, progressive naturally. After she ate, she gave to Adam to eat. After he ate the forbidden fruit, sin, death, and suffering entered the earth.

No one can really say what kind of fruit grew on the tree of knowledge of good and evil. Some say it was an apple because Adam and Eve could bite into it. We can bite into many fruits — peaches, pears, nectarines, and plums to name a few. The actions of Adam brought shame, guilt, separation, and exclusion (Genesis 2:16-17; 3:1-24). When God asked him, "Where art thou?" Adam blamed the woman. When we do things we should not do, stop blaming others. We blame others so that we can continue doing wrong instead of looking at ourselves as the one in control. Once we realize we are in control, it will be easier to take authority over what has taken authority over us.

GENESIS 2:16-17; 3:1-24

We should never blame anyone for something we have done. We should have more control over what we say and what we do. Others should not have any influence on our actions. We must examine ourselves and if there is anything that is not right, we should get rid of it. Those words are easier said than done. Some of us are doing what we were taught in our family circle. We must ask the Lord to help us, because only He can. It is by grace that we can change. This is the reason why the second Adam (Jesus Christ) came to redeem us back to God. We cannot do it through our own strength.

The Tree of Life has 12 varieties of fruits; it symbolizes eternal life. It produces a new fruit every month. God gave

Adam and Eve a choice. He wanted them to make the right decision because He gave them free will. They were able to get food from this tree until they chose to disobey God (Genesis 2:16-17; 3:22-24). Revelation 22:2 *"...the tree of life, producing twelve fruits, yielding its fruit each month; and the leaves of the tree are for the healing of the nations."*

GENESIS 2:16-17; 3:22-24

This one tree of life grows on two sides of the river like a vine that spreads along the flow of the water of life. This tree fulfills what God intended from the beginning. It was closed to man because of the fall of man but it was opened to the believers through the redemption of Christ.

REV. 22:2

The fruits of the tree are the food God redeemed for eternity. With a new fruit each month, it is always fresh. The leaves of the tree of life are for the healing of the nations and symbolize the deeds of Christ. In the Word of God, leaves are a symbol of man's deeds The born-again believers — those who are regenerated — eat the fruit receiving Christ as their inward life and life supply that they may enjoy the divine life of eternity; whereas the restored nations are healed by the leaves of the tree. God's redeemed carry His anointing to heal the sick today.

In Luke 4:18-19 Jesus stood up and said, *"The Spirit of the Lord is upon me, because he hath anointed me to preach the gospel to the poor; he hath sent me to heal the*

LUKE 4:18-19

brokenhearted, to preach deliverance to the captives, and
recovering of sight to the blind, to set at liberty them that
are bruised, To preach the acceptable year of the Lord."

The Anointing

God has given man a measure of the anointing. Every child of God is responsible for maintaining and developing the levels of the anointing. Some walk in a greater anointing than others. According to Ezekiel 47:3-5, we will find that the water was ankle deep, then knee deep, then waist deep, and then it was so deep one had to swim in it.

EZEKIEL 47:3-5

There are levels or degrees of the anointing. The amount of time we spend in the presence of the Lord will determine the degree of the anointing in which we walk. People who have ever worked in ministry know and recognize those who walk in a greater anointing.

In the Old Testament God instructed Moses to use the best spices and a hin of olive oil. He told him that he shall make from these a holy anointing oil. (Exodus 30:22-25) The four spices are myrrh, cinnamon, calamus (or cane), and cassia. Following is an example of where each of the spices and the hin of olive oil came from and how they relate to us spiritually as documented at www.latter-rain.com.

EXODUS 30:22-25

Myrrh is a pale yellow substance or liquid from a small thorny shrub, which grows in Somalia, Ethiopia, and Arabia.

It is used for spice or as an ointment. It is also used as a balm to relief sore parts on the body.

The first thing God wants to do in an individual, so that he can be used as a vessel of honor, is to bring out the spiritual myrrh to purify the vessel. (II Timothy 2:20-21) Some vessels are gold and silver, which represents honor while others are wooden and earthen which represents dishonor. Divine nature (gold) and the redeemed and regenerated human nature (silver) make up honorable vessels. Fallen human nature (wood and earth) make up dishonorable vessels. The vessels that allow God to purify them through Holy Spirit will experience bitterness (do not stay there), but in the end will become a sweet fragrance in God's nostrils. Therefore, myrrh purifies us as a result of us allowing God to cleanse our lives.

II TIMOTHY 2:20-21

The Cinnamon tree grows in Ceylon. Its oil is distilled from the bark of the tree. Because it has a pleasant aroma and pleasant taste, it is used to flavor food.

One of God's requirements for us is that we would be obedient. Obedience is better than sacrifice. 1 Samuel 15:22 says, "... *to obey is better than sacrifice* ..." When we worship, praise, and offer up sacrifices unto the Lord, we must be sure that our lives line up with His Word. Otherwise, we remain stagnant and unfruitful.

I SAMUEL 15:22

We must stop settling for mediocrity. Our decision to do

what is right carries a price. Some people in our lives — those so called "friends" — may not want to be around us anymore. As long as we do what they want us to do, as long as we go where they want us to go, they remain our friends. The price we pay for doing what God says rather than what man says may include feeling misunderstood and rejected. This is the cost of the sweet spiritual cinnamon. Obedience releases cinnamon. Greater rewards await us at the end.

Calamus is a sweet cane plant of about ten feet high. It grows in marshy, soggy, muddy, and wet places in Asia. When it is broken and crushed, it gives off a sweet fragrance. Calamus — brokenness.

ISAIAH 66:2

Isaiah 66:2 says, "*For all those things hath mine hand made, and those things have been, saith the LORD: but to this man will I look, even to him that is poor and of a contrite spirit, and trembleth at my word.*" The word contrite in Hebrew is "*nakeh*" which is an adjective (Strongs 5223) that means smitten. A second word "*dakah*" is a verb (Strongs 1794) meaning to crumble, to bruise, and to break into pieces. We must pass through the stage of brokenness. If we do not, we will continue to walk in the same area, on the same level, never to go higher.

A woman came into the house where Jesus was visiting Simon the leper. She carried an alabaster box that contained very expensive and rare oil extracted from a variety of bearded grasses growing in India. The woman spent years earning the equivalent of three hundred days of labor from merchants who came to her village only once a year to buy the oil, which she was keeping to anoint her bridegroom on their wedding day. The Bible says she broke the box and poured the oil on Jesus' head. (According to Matthew and Mark, she poured it on his head. Luke's account was different: she stood at His feet and cried as she washed his feet with tears, wiped His feet with the hair on her head, kissed His feet and then anointed them.) She gave Jesus the most precious and valuable thing she possessed. She did not care what others thought; she did what she believed was necessary. We must be willing to get rid of our pride if our lives are to be pleasurable and acceptable to carry God's anointing. Pride prevents us from experiencing brokenness.

PRIDE

Job Chapter 41 says Leviathan reigns supreme over all the pride of the earth. All who tolerate pride in their lives become servants of Leviathan — a wreathed animal such as a serpent, crocodile, or large sea monster that speaks about Satan himself, wreathed with the scales of pride.

> JOB
> CHAPTER 41

Isaiah 27:1 says, *"In that day the LORD with his sore and great and strong sword shall punish Leviathan the*

> ISAIAH 27:1

piercing serpent, even leviathan that crooked serpent; and he shall slay the dragon that is in the sea." Only God can deal with this spirit. I have learned when dealing with the spirit of Leviathan that I must focus on God and what He is able to do in my life, rather than the arrogance in which some men and women operate. In Job 41:1 states that when Leviathan is roused he grows ferocious and no one can face him in a fight.

JOB 41:1

When one is anointed he is rubbed with the very presence of God but when one allows pride in his heart he is rubbed with the scales of Leviathan, which are:

- **Pride:** high or inordinate opinion of one's own dignity, importance, merit, or superiority, whether as cherished in the mind or as displayed in bearing, conduct, etc.
- **Arrogance:** offensive display of superiority of self-importance; overbearing pride.
- **Manipulation:** shrewd or devious management, especially for one's own advantage.
- **Domination:** rule or sway; control, often arbitrary.

- **Rebellion:** resistance to or defiance of any authority, control, or tradition; the sin of witchcraft.
- **Contention:** a dispute where there is strong disagreement always disagreeable, causing conflict, and having strife toward others.
- **Boast:** speak of oneself with excessive pride to impress others.
- **Haughtiness:** overbearing pride evidenced by a superior manner toward inferiors.
- **Witchcraft:** magical or irresistible influence, attraction, or charm; misuse of spiritual power to control others.
- **Stubbornness:** difficult to handle or overcome; wanting things our way.

Some of these scales lead to or are accompanied by other conditions. For example: Fear is a companion of pride. One who is proud also has fear in his life. One who leans totally upon the Lord is not afraid. FEAR is false evidence appearing real. Stubbornness leads to rebellion, rebellion leads to pride, and pride leads to destruction.

The strength of Leviathan resides in its neck. When someone is stubborn (stiff-necked) Satan controls his strength, and the flow of God's anointing in his life begins to be dry.

If we have gray areas in our lives, God speaks to us many times so that we might make readjustments and repent. If we disobey and become stiff-necked, it leads us to rebel, opening the door for Leviathan to sow the seed of pride. When pride's seed is fully grown, the scales start to grow and destruction begins. The Bible says in Proverbs 29:23, "*A man's pride shall bring him low: but honour shall uphold the humble in spirit.*"

PROVERBS 29:23

I would rather obey God than man. I am not afraid of what man can do to me. Once we take our eyes off of man, God steps in and takes over our lives. His anointing over our lives is our approval; His favor will be upon us. When we walk in humility, we walk in the anointing and the yoke will be broken in our lives.

Cassia is derived from a Hebrew root word "quadad" meaning to bend, to bow, or to stoop. It is the aromatic bark of a tree growing in Arabia. Some doctors use it as medicine. I Peter 5:6-7 says, "*Humble yourselves therefore under the mighty hand of God, that he may exalt you in due time: Casting all your care upon him; for he careth for you.*"

I PETER 5:6-7

Pride is not an influence; it is a demon spirit trying to destroy the lives of God's people. Submission is the path to humility and humility is the path to promotion. A continuous walk in humility will cause a double portion of God's anointing to flow in our lives.

Why talk about in conjunction with trees? Because pride gets in the way of what God is trying to do in our lives. We do not grow and expand and we surely do not take root in a firm foundation if we are walking in pride. If the trees typify Jesus Christ, then it shows that we were created to be just like Him. The more we take on our Father's characteristics, the more we will become just like Him. There is a release that must take place and it starts when we surrender. We must grow and progress and expand, just like trees. Cassia comes out when we submit to the Lord.

Hin of Olive Oil is one of the components of the sacred anointing oil. Olives, one of the main crops of ancient Israel, were picked in November and pressed between stone wheels to extract the oil. The oil ran into stone vats where it was left to settle and clear. Olive trees take two years to mature and can survive long periods of drought.

In Matthew 4:1-2 it says, *"Then was Jesus led up of the Spirit into the wilderness to be tempted of the devil. And when he had fasted forty days and forty nights, he was afterward an hungred."* Forty has a spiritual meaning — probation and trial. The oil from the olives speaks of probation by trial. After Jesus completed His time of probation

MATTHEW 4:1-2

by trial in the wilderness, He came out victorious. We, too, will be tried and placed under pressure; how we handle it will determine our outcome. Just as olives are processed to get the olive oil, we, too, go through a process to produce the anointing.

Chapter Three
Bitter Waters

(Exodus 15:23-26)

(A statute and an ordinance were given.)

"And when they came to Marah, they could not drink of the waters of Marah, for they were bitter: therefore the name of it was called Marah. And the people murmured against Moses, saying, What shall we drink? And he cried unto the LORD; and the LORD shewed him a tree, which when he had cast into the waters, the waters were made sweet: there he made for them a statute and an ordinance, and there he proved them, And said, If thou wilt diligently hearken to the voice of the LORD thy God, and wilt do that which is right in his sight, and wilt give ear to his commandments, and keep all his statutes, I will put none of these diseases upon thee, which I have brought upon the Egyptians: for I am the LORD that healeth thee."

EXODUS 15:23-26

Moses was leading the Israelites into the promise land. They came from Egypt, where they were getting food and water. When they came to a place where the water was bitter, they started complaining like some of us do when things are not the way we think they should be. Instead of going to the Lord and praying the scriptures, we complain. We call this person and that person. Almost every time we open our mouths, we tell someone about it. However, Moses sought the Lord on behalf of the Israelites and God instructed him to throw a tree into the waters (something simple). The waters became sweet and they were able to drink. At that point a statute and an ordinance were declared. Pay attention very closely because this is a requirement.

If we listen diligently, not just hear, the voice of the LORD our God, and will do that which is right in His sight, and will open our ears to His commandments, and keep all his statutes; He will put none of the diseases, which were brought on the Egyptians, on us: for He is the LORD that will heal us.

We have all found ourselves in a place where, in spite of everything around us, nothing could satisfy us or, if it did, it was not from God. We knew that it was there to please our flesh only and that it was not eternal. It was temporal. We have all been thirsty but nothing we drank that could quench our thirst. Jesus Christ is the only one who can quench our thirst. Nothing will satisfy us until we realize that Christ is the answer.

There is a well that never runs dry and will cause us to no

longer thirst. In the New Testament, a Samaritan woman saw Jesus sitting at Jacob's well with nothing to draw in the water. She asked Him if He was greater than Jacob because Jacob gave the Samaritans the well. Jacob, his children, and his cattle drank from that well. Now keep in mind that Jews did not talk to Samaritans back then. Jesus told her that whoever drank the water from the well would thirst again. However, those who drank of the water Jesus had will cause a well of water to spring up forever. Jesus told the Samaritan woman about her personal life. He told her that she had been married five times and the one she was with was not her husband. She was so amazed that Jesus knew her and her background that she went and told the men of the city, "come see a man." (John 4:1-43) She knew after meeting Jesus that she would no longer thirst after the things that pleased only the flesh. The water that Jesus has will cause us to thirst no more; it is a spring that never dries up. Without it we will go through life looking for something that we will never find in man or woman or in what we do.

JOHN 4:1-43

Throughout the Word of God we find that if we abide by the decrees, regulations, and laws of God, we will have longer days on the earth and many good things will come to us. One statute is to fear the Lord, and another is to sing aloud unto Him, who is our strength: make a joyful noise unto the God of Jacob. Sing a psalm while playing an instrument. There are many, many more.

Following are the Ten Commandments and the Great Commandments.

TEN COMMANDMENTS

Exodus 20:

EXODUS 20:

4, "*Thou shalt not make unto thee any graven image, or any likeness of any thing that is in heaven above, or that is in the earth beneath, or that is in the water under the earth*:

5, "*Thou shalt not bow down thyself to them, nor serve them: for I the LORD thy God am a jealous God, visiting the iniquity of the fathers upon the children unto the third and fourth generation of them that hate me*;

7, "*Thou shalt not take the name of the LORD thy God in vain; for the LORD will not hold him guiltless that taketh his name in vain.*

10, "*But the seventh day is the Sabbath of the LORD thy God: in it thou shalt not do any work, thou, nor thy son, nor thy daughter, thy manservant, nor thy maidservant, nor thy cattle, nor thy stranger that is within thy gates*:

13, "*Thou shalt not kill.*

14, "*Thou shalt not commit adultery.*

15, "*Thou shalt not steal.*

16, "*Thou shalt not bear false witness against thy neighbour.*

17, "*Thou shalt not covet thy neighbour's house, thou shalt not covet thy neighbour's wife, nor his manservant, nor his maidservant, nor his ox, nor his ass, nor any thing that is thy neighbour's.*"

THE GREAT COMMANDMENTS

> MATTHEW
> 22:36-40

The Great Commandments in the law are found in Matthew 22:36-40. When a disciple asked which is the great commandment, Jesus answered, *Thou shalt love the Lord thy God with all thy heart, and with all thy soul, and with all thy mind. This is the first and great commandment. The second is like unto it, thou shalt love thy neighbour as thyself.*

All the law and prophets hang on these two commandments. The first four of the Ten Commandments, fall under the first Great Commandment. The remainder of the Ten Commandments falls under the second Great

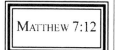

MATTHEW 7:12

Commandment. The Golden Rule — Do unto others as you would have them do unto you — also has its roots in the Bible. Matthew 7:12 says, *"Therefore all things whatsoever ye would that men should do to you, do ye even so to them: for this is the law and the prophets."*

People sometimes do not treat themselves right so they mistreat others. We must examine our hearts and pray. We must ask the Lord to cleanse us and make our hearts whiter than snow. In doing this, we will know that what comes from the heart reaches the heart. The issues of life come from the heart through our mouths and manifest around us.

I was in a grocery store one early Saturday morning. There was an elderly man bent over in line with his small amount of groceries in his cart. I had about $50.00 worth of groceries in my cart. He looked at me and said hard times are coming. If this man had been looking at life from a different perspective, he would have excelled. Many great doors would have opened for him. I told him I would not agree with him. If we keep saying negative comments about life, we will get whatever we say. I told him to start saying, "I have more than enough." I mentioned to him to give to others, which will also cause God's word to manifest in his life. Give and it shall be given unto you press down, shaken together and running over shall men give unto our bosoms. God honors His Word. As the rain comes down and it snows from heaven, so shall His Word be that comes out of His mouth. It will not return to Him void.

I will always say for the rest of my life, "I am a money magnet. Money comes to me. I will never be broke another day in my life." The Bible says, we shall decree a thing and it shall be established.

What we say and do to others is very important. I told my children that whatever they say out of their mouths about others would come back to them. If they mistreat anyone, it will come back to them in a different form.

According to Deuteronomy 6:5-8, we will love the Lord with all our hearts, soul and might; we will know the first Great Commandment will be in our hearts; we will teach our children diligently; we will talk about it in our homes (in the morning, in the noon day, and even at night), while we are walking around, when we lay down, and even when we get up. We will carry it around, and it will even be before us.

DEUTERONOMY
6:5-8

Chapter Four
Is It An Orange Or An Apple?

(Song of Solomon 2: 3)

"As the apple tree among the trees of the wood, so is my beloved among the sons. I sat down under his shadow with great delight, and his fruit was sweet to my taste."

SOLOMON 2:3

Solomon wrote the Song of Solomon ("Song of Songs"). The songs sung as a play. He wrote two other songs in Psalms 72 and 127 (He also wrote the book of Proverbs that compares a foolish man to a wise man.) The Song of Songs teaches us about a relationship between a man and a woman. However, it is necessary to note that this particular book is about the mutual love of Christ and His Church, a love so awesome that He gave His life for it.

PSALMS 72 & 127

This relationship, which the Shulamite woman had with Solomon, was very poetic. All of us have met someone that flowed rhythmically with us. It seemed as if everything was in sync. The love was so great that we knew how each other felt before we either spoke. One could start a sentence and the other would finish it. He/she knew exactly what the other wanted to say. We would be in two different places getting ready to call one another; the phone would ring and it would be the other person.

While reading the Song of Songs, picture the wonderful relationship Solomon had with the Shulamite woman. Her parents were responsible for Solomon's vineyard. When her father passed she had to do most of the work. While she was working in the vineyard, King Solomon saw her, developed a love for her, and promised he would marry her. Solomon kept his promise. Single women who anticipate getting married must know that Solomon could be watching. If we are wise, we will get to know each other before we get married and consummate the wedding ceremony. Keep in mind, throughout the years of marriage unexpected situations happen where we must be strong and endure in order to keep the marriage vows.

Marriage is sacred between a man and a woman. God designed marriage for us. Solomon teaches us about the purity and faithfulness of the God-given institution. Sexual love should be pure between a man and his wife. Whenever one goes outside the marriage for sexual pleasure it defiles the sanctity of the marriage.

The Shulamite spoke out about what she wanted, how she wanted to be comforted; she knew what she needed. She believed he was the only one who could meet her needs. Some women frequently change their minds because they do not know what they want or need. Other women know what they want and realize that Jesus is the only one that can meet their needs. I am in the second group. Jesus is the only one who satisfies me. I have searched, and searched, and searched, and realize that Christ came to give me all I need. What I need and desire is in me already.

It's easy to become frustrated when we look on the outside for what is already inside each of us because the outside cannot compare to what we have had inside from the beginning.

Relationships are important to the Father horizontally and vertically. He desires that we walk together and agree on the same thing. Amos 3:3 asks, "*Can two walk together except they be agreed*." We cannot agree to disagree when it comes to God. This is compromising and going along with what is wrong. We must choose our battles carefully. We should keep unity among us. Everyone does not worship the Lord the same but that does not mean it is wrong. We all are worshipping a common denominator: God whom we know by many names including:

AMOS 3:3

- The Creator, The Judge (*Elohim* — el-o-heem')

- The All-Sufficient One, the Lord God Almighty (*El Shaddai* — el shad-dï)
- The Most High God (*El Elyon* — el el-yone')
- Lord, Master (*Adonai* — ad-o-noy')
- Lord, Jehovah (*Yahweh* or *Jehovah* — yah-weh)
- The Lord My Banner, The Lord My Miracle (*Jehovah Nissi* — yeh-ho-vaw' nis-see')
- The Lord My Shepherd (*Jehovah-Raah* — yeh-ho-vaw' raw'aw')
- The Lord That Heals (*Jehovah-Rapha* — yeh-ho-vaw' raw-faw')
- The Lord is There (*Jehovah-Shammah* — yeh-ho-vaw' shawn'-maw)
- The Lord Our Righteousness (*Jehovah Tsidkenu* — yeh-ho-vaw' tsid-kay'-noo)
- The Lord Who Sanctifies You, The Lord Who Makes Holy (*Jehovah Mekoddishkem* — yeh-ho-vaw' M-qadash)
- The Everlasting God, The God of Eternity, The God of the Universe, The

God of Ancient Days (*El Olam* — el o-lawm')

- Jealous, Zealous (*Qanna* — kan-naw')
- The Lord Will Provide (*Jehovah Jireh* — yeh-ho-vaw' yir-eh')
- The Lord is Peace (*Jehovah-Shalom* — yeh-ho-vaw' shaw-lome')
- The Lord of Powers, The Lord of Hosts (*Jehovah Sabaoth* — yeh-ho-vaw' se ba' br)

He is our strength, a very present help in a time of trouble. He is our refuge. His truth is our shield and buckler. We must walk in the Word of God. We must make His oracles (God's spoken Word) flow from the depths of our bellies out of our mouths and form our world around us. It will cause us to give thanks in everything. Isaiah 55:12 says, "*For ye shall go out with joy, and be led forth with peace: the mountains and the hills shall break forth before you into singing, and all the trees of the field shall clap their hands.*" We must make His Word manifest in the lives of those to whom we talk to. We must agree that God is the All-sufficient One.

ISAIAH 55:12

Unity is power. If we can find someone who thinks the same thing we do, we will have power in that thing whether it is good or evil. Gang members join together to create more gang violence. Everything they try to accomplish is not all bad; it's just that they're involved in more negative than positive dealings. People of God should be of one accord to cause the things of God to manifest on the earth. It often seems that people who do wrong prosper more than people who do good, but things are not always the way they appear. Our imaginations can take us places others could never fathom. They can bring us into situations that are not really happening. We can look at something one way and perceive it to be another way.

Some people generally believe that other people think the same way they do, which is not true. Since people think differently because of their background, culture, likes and dislikes, and upbringing, no two minds think alike all the time. That does not mean that they are right or wrong; it means they have their own point of view. People are individuals and we were created so uniquely that even our fingerprints are different. No two people have the same fingerprints. Those in the business of counterfeit have discovered ways to duplicate originals. It might appear right but it is not.

Evil is a perversion of what is good. The spirit of deception, which looks right, will mislead us into thinking that it is the right thing and correct way to go. But in time we realize that is not the case.

THE RIDE FROM HELL

I realized one day that I had been riding on a bus that was going around and around and around. I needed a particular person to pay attention to me. While riding this bus, I could only look out the window, wondering and hoping that my true love would be at the predetermined stop when the bus arrived; he wasn't. I asked the driver to keep going not caring that others were waiting to get on or off; I didn't want to be late getting to the next stop where my true love might be waiting. I heard something ticking and looked at my watch then realized it was not my watch, but my heart. I believed my love would be at the next stop; all that mattered was that I get to that stop. I really wanted to get off that bus so that I could move on with my life.

When we got to the next stop, my true love was not there, so I asked the bus driver to keep going. Eventually we came to a fork in the road. The bus driver asked, "Now which route do you think we should take?" I wasn't sure. If I chose one route he might be on the other. I had been riding this bus for at least twenty-five years. ... *I am so confused ... I am so confused. I should really be tired by now. As a matter of fact, I am exhausted. If I do not make a decision, I will be here for the rest of my life. I must go on and stop focusing and wondering whether my true love will meet me like he said he would.*

I needed to walk in my vision and stop being concerned about meeting my true love. If my true love could not meet me and look me in the eyes, he did not want to follow my vision. I decided I would focus on how I will love the next person and not how they will love me.

Vision determines our paths. If we do not know where we are going, it does not matter what road we take. If our vision is not His vision then we are on the wrong bus. Vision weeds out those who are not good for us, it gives us limitations on what we will and will not accept, and it attracts those that want to follow the same vision.

We cannot assume anything from a relationship. We cannot let our imaginations run wild. We must not jump to conclusions. We must stop hearing what we want to hear and listen to what is really being said. We want honesty. We only want the truth. If a person can tell us the truth, then we know that they are true to themselves. If a person lies to us, then they are really lying to themselves. We must protect our hearts. If a person does not view another as a future asset, then most likely he/she does not want to marry the other.

We can be trapped in our own worlds, our own minds,

which will consume our thoughts. There are many things going on around us that are just as important as what we are thinking about, for instance, helping others. When our focus is on helping someone else, it makes us feel better. We should not neglect what is important in our lives, however, helping others has its rewards, but we should not help others because we are looking for something in return. Our focus should be on helping meet the needs of others. Life is more fulfilling when we help meet the need of others. If we want something more out of life, help others fulfill their dreams. Vision takes us into another world. Habakkuk 2:2-4 tells us to write the vision clearly enough so that when others read it, they will run with it.

> HABAKKUK
> 2:2-4

Prepare first. There is always a season of preparation. Count up the cost; get estimates. We must plan our lives and to allow room for the Spirit of the Lord to come in and push back *Chronos* time so that *Kairos* time can step in and cause God's plan for our lives to manifest. Chronos is defined as "time indefinitely or a certain time, period, season or space of time — twenty-four hours in a day, seven days a week, twelve months in a year." In Chronos time, our walk with the Lord is characterized by our daily faithfulness and obedience to follow His voice.

Change is measured as we look back over our lives and see how the Lord's hand has guided us faithfully one step at a time. At specific times in history, God suddenly and sovereignly stepped from eternity into the earthly timeline to affect His perfect plan and purposes. Normal rules that govern time and change are suspended. His supernatural becomes our natural. The intersection of eternity and earthly time produces sudden acceleration that propels us forward into His purpose.

Kairos means "the right season, the right time for action, and the critical moment." (www.lsm.org — Watchman Nee) We have all heard, "I was in the right place at the right time, or I was in the wrong place at the wrong time."

We can choose to obey or disobey the voice of the Lord. However, when Kairos time comes into motion nothing we can do or say can prevent the plan and purpose of God for our lives. His will shall be done. He designed us with a purpose in mind. God knew us before He placed us in our mother's womb. He took care of us when we were just a thought in His mind. He always had us on His mind, to prosper us. He has already equipped us to be successful.

We must stay focused and study God's Word, which is a road map through life. It will take us through the journey of life in the right direction.

CHAPTER FIVE
THE STEM OF JESSE

(Isaiah 11:1)

ISAIAH 11:1

"And there shall come forth a rod out of the stem of Jesse, and a Branch shall grow out of his roots:"

Let's focus on that. A twig will come forth from the stem of Jesse, and a branch from his roots will bear fruit. The root of David or the stem of Jesse is referring to a righteous branch — Jesus Christ. The colon at the end of the verse above is an indication that something will happen when the rod comes out of the stem of Jesse the branch will grow out. Isaiah 11:2-4 tells us that the spirit of the Lord shall rest upon us, the spirit of wisdom, the spirit of counsel and might, the spirit of knowledge and the fear of the Lord. We will have quick understanding in the fear of the Lord and shall not judge others by what we see but will judge with righteousness. Our words will destroy the earth and our breath will slay the wicked.

ISAIAH 11:2-4

The stem of Jesse and the root of David are terms used for the Messiah (Isaiah 11:10; Rev. 5:5). Roots of a tree must

ISAIAH 11:10;
REV. 5:5

be deep enough and strong enough to give strength to the tree. If the roots are damaged, the tree will not grow properly. In fact it will die.

1 TIMOTHY 6:10

The root of any source that is not good will not survive. 1 Timothy 6:10 says, *"For the love of money is the root of all evil: which while some coveted after, they have erred from the faith, and pierced themselves through with many sorrows."* This scripture does not say money is evil. It says the love of money is evil. When we love money more than anything, we do things that are not right. We do not think clearly our focus is only on money. Money should not rule us. If we desire to receive good gifts, our focus should be on things above and the Lord's righteousness and all earthly things shall be added unto us. Many people fall into traps that are difficult to get out of when they let money rule them. This represents the source of a situation.

PROVERBS 12:3

According to Solomon, the root of righteous establishes us and nothing will be able to move us. Proverbs 12:3 says, *"A man shall not be established by wickedness: but the root of the righteous shall not be moved."* This represents stability. When a tree's roots are strong, the tree grows tall and the branches spread wide. Solomon also speaks about the root of righteousness producing fruit. Proverbs 12:12 says,

PROVERBS 12:12

"The wicked desireth the net of evil men: but the root of

the righteous yieldeth fruit." The increase of fruit represents prosperity. It may seem as if the wicked prospers, but if we wait long enough, we will see the wicked fall right before our eyes.

The bloodline that Jesus came through was the son of Abraham, the son of David. In Matthew 1:1-16 it tells us who begot whom. We are able to see the lineage of Jesus. It is very important as a family that we keep up with who is in our family. Listed are the generations of Jesus.

MATTHEW 1:1-16

"*Abraham begat Isaac; and Isaac begat Jacob; and Jacob begat Judas and his brethren; And Judas begat Phares and Zara of Thamar; and Phares begat Esrom; and Esrom begat Aram; And Aram begat Aminadab; and Aminadab begat Naasson; and Naasson begat Salmon; And Salmon begat Booz of Rachab; and Booz begat Obed of Ruth; and Obed begat Jesse; And Jesse begat David the king; and David the king begat Solomon of her that had been the wife of Urias; And Solomon begat Roboam; and Roboam begat Abia; and Abia begat Asa; And Asa begat Josaphat; and Josaphat begat Joram; and Joram begat Ozias; And Ozias begat Joatham; and Joatham begat Achaz; and Achaz begat Ezekias; And Ezekias begat Manasses; and Manasses begat Amon; and Amon begat Josias; And Josias begat Jechonias and his brethren, about the time they were carried away to Babylon: And after they were brought to Babylon, Jechonias begat Salathiel; and Salathiel begat Zorobabel; And Zorobabel begat Abiud; and Abiud begat Eliakim; and Eliakim begat Azor; And Azor begat Sadoc; and Sadoc begat Achim; and Achim begat Eliud; And Eliud begat Eleazar; and Eleazar begat Matthan; and Matthan begat Jacob; And Jacob begat Joseph the husband of Mary, of whom was born Jesus, who is called Christ. So all the generations from Abraham to David are fourteen generations; and from David until the carrying away into Babylon are fourteen generations; and from the carrying away into Babylon unto Christ are fourteen generations."*

I KINGS 8:65

In dreams the number fourteen is significant. "And at that time Solomon held a feast ... before the Lord our God, seven days and seven days, even fourteen days." (I Kings 8:65) on page ninety-six of Understanding the Dreams you Dream by: Ira Milligan, we find that fourteen means double, recreate, reproduce, disciple, servant and bond slave (employee).

Jesus came to serve us. He did not think about what He was giving up; He thought about His mission. Even when He was in the Garden of Gethsemane, He said nevertheless.... He wanted us to be recreated in God's imagine after His likeness. Whatever it took, He was willing to do. He came and taught the disciples how to be disciples. It was already in them; Jesus brought it out. Our goal should be to help others get to their destiny no matter what we have to give up. We should want to see everyone in the place they were originally ordained to be. When we are on a mission, it does not matter who we like or dislike. What really matters is that we be about our Father's business. He employed us to perform a task to get the job done. Reach out and love just like Jesus did. The end of John 14 says, " … *Arise, let us go hence.*" Once we learn to love unconditionally, we will see clearly and will go from that place to a higher place.

Before Joseph and Mary were intimate, she was pregnant with the child of the Holy Ghost. Joseph was going to put her away so that the public would not find out. While he was thinking, the angel of the Lord appeared in a dream, calling him the son of David. He said not to be afraid and to take Mary to be his wife. The Holy Spirit said, "for that which is conceived in her is of the Holy Ghost." He instructed Joseph to call his son Jesus and told him that Jesus shall save his people from their sins. The prophecy was fulfilled at this time, which was spoken by the prophet Isaiah. The Prophet Isaiah decreed that the child would be named Emmanuel, which means God with us. Joseph took Mary to be his wife and did not touch her until she birthed her son. When Mary delivered, Joseph called his name Jesus.

If the people then were like the people today, they were undoubtedly talking about the color of her wedding dress; some were probably saying she couldn't, wear all white because only women who are virgins wear white on their wedding day. What they did not know was that even, after baby Jesus was conceived, Mary still was a virgin. Matthew 1:25 says, *"And knew her not till she had brought forth her firstborn son: ..."*

Matthew 1:25

Jesus came to save us, to give us abundant life. He came to redeem our relationship with the Father so that we would walk in divine life. When we look at the world, it often seems others are having a better time than we are. We have to make up in our minds whether we are going to serve God or man. When we realize that our relationship with Christ is worth more than anything, we will walk in abundant life. We will know that the spirit of deception is making it seem as though the world is having a better time.

Abundant life means every one of our needs should be met. We should also receive the desires of our hearts. Our needs met and receiving the desires of our hearts reveals that we are walking in the land flowing with milk and honey. Milk represents our needs being met and honey represents us receiving the desires of our hearts. In Matthew chapter 6 we find that we are not to worry about tomorrow because tomorrow will take care of itself. We should not worry about what we are going to eat, drink, or wear. If He thinks more highly of us than the birds of the air and the lilies in the field, why should we worry?

The Lord has plans for our lives. Jeremiah 29:11 tells us, "*For I know the thoughts that I think toward you, saith the LORD, thoughts of peace, and not of evil, to give you an expected end.*" Once we believe that He can do anything but fail and that there is nothing too hard for Him, we will put all our trust in the Lord. We must seek after wisdom and understanding, in order to obtain great wealth.

JEREMIAH 29:11

According to Isaiah 9:6 Jesus' name should be called " *... Wonderful, Counselor, The Mighty God, The Everlasting Father, and The Prince of Peace.*" These are five attributes of Jesus. Five is the number of grace. It is because of Christ that God's grace is sufficient.

ISAIAH 9:6

Chapter Six
The Storm

(Isaiah 25:4)

"*For thou hast been a strength to the poor, a strength to the needy in his distress, a refuge from the storm, a shadow from the heat, when the blast of the terrible ones is as a storm against the wall.*"

The tilt of the earth's axis is responsible for our seasons. During the summer the sun's rays hit the earth at a more direct angle than they do in winter. In the Northern Hemisphere, the winter solstice is the day when the sun is farthest south or December 21. In the Southern Hemisphere, winter and summer solstices are reversed so that the winter solstices is the day on which the sun is farthest north or June 21. Day and night are equal on the spring — vernal — equinox (March 21 in the Northern Hemisphere or September 21 in the Southern Hemisphere and the fall —autumnal — equinox September 21 in the Northern Hemisphere or March 21 in the Southern Hemisphere).

Just as there are different seasons on earth, we go through different seasons in our lives. Certain situations come in the spring, a time when budding starts. Others are in the summer, a time of full bloom. Our surroundings change during the fall, a time of preparation for the winter. Some think change is not good, but the opposite is true. God gives us instructions and warnings in the fall; if we do not heed them, we will not be ready for winter, a time of hibernation when things seem to move slower or go dormant. Circumstances — good or bad — are at their fullest when they affect us most. In bad situations when it seems we are going to break into pieces Jesus is in control of our lives. He will take that bad situation and turn it around for our good. The sun will shine.

PROVERBS 30: 25, 26, 27, 28

In the summer ants work to store food for winter. In Proverbs 30: 25, Solomon speaks of the ants preparing their meat in the summer even though they are not strong. In Proverbs 30:26, conies are feeble insects, yet they know to find shelter in rocks. In Proverbs 30:27, locusts have no ruler, yet they know there is unity in numbers. In Proverbs 30:28, the spider takes hold with her hands, and is in kings' palaces. The insects know what to do to prepare, unite, excel, and find shelter.

Farmers also know there is a time to sow and a time to harvest crops. If they plant at the wrong time, the crops will not grow.

We must learn how to manage and take care of ourselves in any given situation. Learn to sit quietly and listen to the sound of nothing. At times in life we are constantly moving, talking, and listening to many different things. We need to heed the advice of "*... be still ...*" Mark 4:39. If we turn off the radio and the television, get in a quiet place, and listen we will hear a whole lot.

MARK 4:39

Hurricane Katrina struck in September 2005 destroying much of New Orleans, Louisiana; she also caused lesser destruction in neighboring areas of Louisiana and neighboring states. When the levees broke in New Orleans water poured over the land. People climbed on rooftops to get away from the rising waters but many were stranded without food and shelter for days; some died. I heard rumors that, the Levees, not strong enough to hold the water back, broke and allowed large amounts of water to flood the land. Many people died because they went days without food and water. Crocodiles came ashore and ate some of the bodies. Some people climbed to the tops of their roofs because the water had gotten so high to have covered all their living spaces.

MATTHEW 16:18

Our support system must be as solid as a rock. Matthew 16:18 says, "*And I say also unto thee, That thou art Peter, and upon this rock I will build my church; and the gates*

PSALMS 107:25, 29

of hell shall not prevail against it." King David says in Psalms 107:25, 29 "*For he commandeth, and raiseth the stormy wind, which lifteth up the waves thereof: He maketh the storm a calm, so that the waves thereof are still.*"

After Hurricane Katrina many people heard devastating stories about friends and relatives. I received an email about a woman who was rescued and taken to a church in Atlanta with her sons. Someone told her that they saw her daughter dead by a store. The woman walked in fear while she lived in New Orleans and when she was leaving for Atlanta. Once in a church in Atlanta, she found out that she did not have the fear anymore. The Lord blessed her with a house; the daughter she thought was dead was brought safely to her. God performed miracle after miracle. Every unexpected blessing made her faith stronger. Today she believes that God can do anything but fail and that there is nothing impossible to those who believe.

ROMANS 8:28

ISAIAH 54:17

Romans 8:28 says, "*... all things work together for good to them that love God, to them who are the called according to his purpose.*" Isaiah 54:17 says, "*No weapon that is formed against thee shall prosper; ...*" We must believe the Word of the Lord. We must stop looking at what is going on around us and put our trust in The One (Jesus) who fixed it in the beginning and everything will work out for our good. This is why we must give thanks no matter what the situation. Today's circumstances or situations should not dictate our tomorrow.

One year I was asked to put together something for the ministers to preach on New Year's Eve to bring in the New Year with a Word from God. I heard the Spirit of the Lord saying that His people were in the midst of storms and that they did not believe that He could bring them out or even protect them from the storm.

I began to write. I gathered all the reading material on storms that I could find in the house. I found information on the storm, the wind, and the rain. I sought the Lord about the order and what He wanted me to do with the information. Days went by. I was in the middle of doing something else when He spoke to me. He told me to get in His presence and seek His face before I did anything else. I remembered getting a pen and paper to write down what He said. As I went into worship (telling God who He is to us) and praise (thanking Him for what He did, is doing, and what He was going to do for us), He spoke to my spirit. He told me to start by preparing an outline. Thirteen ministers were scheduled to speak and a slot opened for one more. That night I also had to cook a couple of dishes for the night service because the ministers not only had to preach and teach they also had to feed the people. Natural food and Spiritual food goes together. The Spirit of the Lord wants to meet every need, not just one. The messages that night were so awesome that the children of God left with hope, feeling that God did not bring them this far to leave them.

When the storm has passed we think of so many things we needed during the storm. We cannot prepare enough for the storms of life. No matter how we prepare, after a disaster hits we always think of things we could have done to survive. God's Survival Kit was created before He formed us in our mother's wombs, before He laid the four corners of the earth, before He laid the foundation of the world. He had a plan; our lives were predestined before we were born. In the book of Jeremiah, God told Jeremiah He knew him before He placed him in his mother's womb.

We need very little to survive some storms while we need to be prepared for the worst in others by having survival items in specific places in our homes or at work. Hurricane Rita followed and did more damage. In 2005, there were so many Hurricanes, the meteorologists were forced to start using Greek names beginning with Alpha — the beginning. A travel agent was concerned about getting to Omega — the end. Think about it; God is Alpha and Omega — the beginning and the end — the first and the last.

In Asia a Tsunami and an earthquake in Pakistan killed thousands. In 2006 the bird flu has spread from Asia to Europe and Africa infecting humans for the first time. Mosquitoes have been spreading the West Nile Virus since 2004. Since we never know when a disaster is going to hit, we need to be prepared. Here is a list of items to have packed and easy to grab when severe weather strikes:

- Light color backpack
- 30-piece first-aid kit
- Tissue
- Nonperishable goods of a 3-day supply of food and water (5 year shelf life)
- Battery operated flashlight
- Battery operated radio
- Extra batteries (whatever the flash light and radio require)
- 12-hour light stick
- Thermal blanket
- Biohazard waste bags
- Bottle of bleach
- Trash bags and duke tape
- Respirator mask
- Whistle
- A plan for the family to communicate
- 1 roll of Home Guard barrier sheeting
- Cell phone

Disasters come in many different forms. They do not have to come from nature. There are financial storms when people cannot get finances in order. There are marital storms where it seems that hell has been loosed on the marriage. There are parental storms when children disobey to the point that they are imprisoned. Some children and adults were victims of mistaken identity because they were in the wrong place at the wrong time. On the other hand, they could be in prison in their minds and thoughts; trapped in a world where they will not listen to what is right.

Storms of life help us realize that we must be strong, must not break under pressure. Remember a set-back is a set-up for a come back. Be strong as the oak and sway like the willow. In other words, "be shrewd as a snake and gentle as a dove." We can do all things in Him who strengthens us. Have you ever been pushed beyond your limits to find that you can do more, go further, and handle any situation? We can be pushed beyond our perceived limits in many situations.

There are times in our lives when God speaks to us by asking a question. He does not expect an answer. He wants to bring something to our attention. He stretches us to do more, to take us to a higher level, a higher dimension. He wants us to see what we are really made of and it is not just sugar and spice and everything nice. We can find great potential in ourselves to discover our purpose. Before our mothers and fathers met, God had us on His mind.

With life's adversities, we must realize that we still have the VICTORY. We are not defeated. We must keep telling ourselves that victory is ours. It was already established before the foundation was laid on the earth. God took care of us when we were just a thought in His mind. He predestined our lives before we came into existence. He knew our ending before He created our beginning: that is why we call Him Alpha and Omega. All power belongs to Him. His word is settled. Do you agree?

Chapter Seven
The True Vine

(John 15:1, 15)

Being connected and not just attached. "*I am the true vine, and My Father is the husbandman. ...Henceforth I call you not servants; for the servant knoweth not what his lord doeth: but I have called you friends; for all things that I have heard of my Father I have made known unto you.*"

JOHN 15:1, 15

I call Jesus the vinedresser. A vinedresser is someone who takes care of the vineyard. Who cultivates the vines to be sure it produces fruit. In the Word of God, we will find grapevines indicating that people ate fresh grapes, or raisins, or used grapes in wine making.

God wants us to be productive. Fruit grows and is given as gifts. He wants us to bear much fruit. Every branch that does not bear fruit, He takes away and every branch He prunes, that it may bear more fruit. We must stay connected in the vine by abiding in Jesus Christ. He is the True Vine; we are the branches. God, the Father, is the husbandman, which is our source. The way we abide in the Lord is to obey His Word. This is what makes us one with Him. Now, He is able to work through us. When we pray, Jesus Christ is jointly praying for us. This is related to fruit bearing and will surely cause our prayers and what Jesus Christ is praying will be answered. Fruit bearing causes God's divine blessing and reward to manifest in our lives. We will hear the Lord clearly and will follow His commandments.

We will see the fruit of the Spirit manifesting. We must choose to allow the fruit to grow in our lives. Situations will come up that will cause the fruit to either grow or never manifest. For instance, self-control — I was in a situation where someone made negative comments toward me. I examined the situation and kept my mouth shut. I continued to walk in love. I heard the Lord saying that when someone is hurting they might say things they do not mean. This helped me identify the spirit behind it. Because I did not add to her anger, I grew the fruit of self-control and her anger towards me disappeared. A soft answer turns away wrath. My silence fell under the category of a soft answer. It is not to say that I will not, at times, forget that I am bearing that piece of fruit. I must adhere to and listen to the voice of the Lord. Every situation is different, however, we must allow the Spirit of the

Lord to move in our lives. It is not by power, nor by might, but it is by the Spirit of the Lord. Not only will we produce fruit when we walk in the fruit of the Spirit, but we will cause it to multiply.

Galatians 5:22-23 says, *"But the fruit of the Spirit is love, joy, peace, longsuffering, gentleness, goodness, faithfulness, meekness, self-control; against such things there is no law."*

> GALATIANS
> 5:22-23

Where are we in each of these? Do we manifest all, one, two, or more?

Walk in **love**. God is love according to 1 John 4: 8. There is no occasion that justifies hating or becoming bitter. Walk in the joy of the Lord because it will strengthen us. We must refuse to be cynical and a lazy thinker. Refuse to degrade people; see them as human beings created by and for God. Look at problems as an opportunity for God to prove Himself strong (El Shaddai).

> 1 JOHN 4: 8.

Walk in **joy**. The joy of the Lord is my strength. When we go through whatever storms are raging around us, we must have the Lord's JOY. His JOY will keep us. His JOY comes no matter what the circumstance. The way to walk in God's JOY is to keep looking toward the hills from where our help comes knowing that all help comes from the Lord.

Walk in **peace**. We must not let the sun go down on our wrath. We must forgive people quickly so that we will not walk in bondage. Peace will set the offender's mind free toward us. We must keep our minds on the Lord because the Bible says we will be at perfect peace Isaiah 26:3 tells us, "*Thou wilt keep him in perfect peace, whose mind is stayed on thee: because he trusteth in thee.*". He will give us peace that surpasses all understanding and cause peace to multiply on the earth. When situations are chaotic, He will change the atmosphere.

ISAIAH 26:3

Walk in **longsuffering**. Psalms 23:4 says, "*Yeah, thou I walk through the valley of the shadow of death, I will fear no evil.*" We are covered going in and covered coming out. We will go through the fiery furnace but know that we will come out pure as gold. Do not give up. Hold on. It is not as bad as it seems.

PSALMS 23:4

Walk in **gentleness**. Have compassion for others. We never know what people went through before they approached us. We need understanding as it says in Proverbs 4:7, "*Wisdom is the principal thing; therefore get wisdom: and with all thy getting get understanding.*" Be thoughtful, considerate, and sympathetic to all people.

PROVERBS 4:7

Walk in **goodness**. Cheating does not pay. We must walk in integrity at all costs. If a cashier gives us more change than he/she should, we need to give back what does not belong to us. Some people take it as a blessing in disguise when actually; they end up losing more than they thought they gained.

Walk in **faithfulness**. Can people count on us? Do we stand behind what we say? Jesus shows us that He walks in faithfulness. He is never late; He will never let us down. Situations arise in our lives where it seems the Lord has forgotten about us. Know this, that He is right there with us, carrying us. He brings us to a place of resting in Him. He said that He would never leave us nor forsake us. Even when we decide to leave Him, and backslide, He is married to the backslider. He goes after the one sheep that runs away from the other ninety-nine.

Walk in **meekness**. We should never force anything to be done. We must humble ourselves and walk in humility. 2 Chronicles 7:14 tells us, if we humble ourselves, seek God's face, turn from our wicked ways, and pray, we will hear from heaven, and God will heal the land. Remember pride comes before a fall.

> 2 CHRONICLES 7:14

Walk in **self-control**. This piece of fruit is one that many Christians lack. If we could only control our behavior and tongue, we would be able to focus on bigger and better things. James Chapter 3 says all creatures can tame their tongues except humans. We must go to God and ask Him to help us.

> JAMES CHAPTER 3

When we do, we will be put in situations that will cause us to check our spirits to see if we are operating in the right spirit.

The works of the flesh are found in Galatians 5:19-21, *"Now the works of the flesh are manifest, which are [these]; Adultery, fornication, uncleanness, lasciviousness, Idolatry, witchcraft, hatred, variance, emulations, wrath, strife, seditions, heresies, Envyings, murders, drunkenness, revellings, and such like: of the which I tell you before, as I have also told [you] in time past, that they which do such things shall not inherit the Kingdom of God."*

God wants His Kingdom to manifest on the earth through us, the saints. Kingdom living is having territory to rule, having dominion and authority over everything upon the Earth.

PSALMS 24:1

Psalms 24:1 says, *"The earth is the LORD's, and the fulness thereof; the world, and they that dwell therein."* God gave the earth to us to live on. His original plan was for us to take care of what He created. We must walk in the spirit in order to produce the necessary fruit so that we can subdue the Earth. This is a mandate. Are we walking in the fruit of the Spirit? Do we desire to? Why not take it to the Lord in prayer right now. If we do so sincerely, He will grant them according to the desires of our hearts.

Chapter Eight
Created To Produce

(Genesis 1:22; 28)

"And God blessed them, saying, Be fruitful, and multiply, and fill the waters in the seas, and let fowl multiply in the earth. ... And God blessed them, and God said unto them, Be fruitful, and multiply, and replenish the earth, and subdue it: and have dominion over the fish of the sea, and over the fowl of the air, and over every living thing that moveth upon the earth."

GENESIS 1:22; 28

God created us in His image, after His likeness Genesis 1:27 tells us that He created every living creature — all the animals, birds of the air, fish of the sea, and insects. He created all creatures to multiply, to produce after their own kind. He is the awesome Creator that only creates originals. We, like animals, have instinct. According to Webster, an instinct (as a noun) is a natural or inherent aptitude, impulse, or capacity; largely inheritable and unalterable tendency of an organism to

GENESIS 1:27

make a complex and specific response to environmental stimuli without involving reason; behavior that is meditated by reactions below the conscious level. Instinct, as an adjective, is impelled by an inner or animating or exciting agency; profoundly imbued (i.e., instill, fill, permeate).

The Creator made us with an inner mechanism that reacts to impulse i.e., a desire, an inclination, and an urge. God also gave each of us vertebrate making us mammals. Humans are members of the class Mammalia, the highest class of Vertebrata or warm-blooded animals that nourish their young with milk secreted by mammary glands, have skin usually more or less covered with hair, and a muscular diaphragm separating the heart and lungs from the abdominal cavity (www.dictionary.com).

Genesis 2:7

In Genesis 2:7, God created man from the dust of the earth and blew His breath into man, and man became a living soul. ("*And the LORD God formed man of the dust of the ground, and breathed into his nostrils the breath of life; and man became a living soul.*") He put man to sleep and

Genesis 2:22-23

performed a spiritual surgery. He opened man's side and took his rib and created woman. In Genesis 2:22-23 it says, "*And the rib, which the LORD God had taken from man, made he a woman, and brought her unto the man. And Adam said, This is now bone of my bones, and flesh of my flesh:*

she shall be called Woman, because she was taken out of Man." Some say God took man's affectionate side, his emotional side from his rib and created woman. I find that men have feelings, too; they hurt and suffer wounded spirits. When I was seeking the Lord, for a Word for men, one year on Fathers' Day, He gave me something that men can ponder in their hearts:

> I, God, designed you in such a way that you are already equipped to have dominion over your household and everything in the earth. I created you before I created woman because you and I have a special connection. I made you in my own image because I knew that just like me, you would visualize something and carry it in your heart and then you would speak great things into existence. Those who have children, you give them their identity by what you speak into their lives and the examples you set. Over time you lost focus and started thinking in your own ability. You stopped looking to Me to make decisions for you. Some of you did not have a father figure to set an example for you, and some had a father living in the home, however, the father did not have a relationship with Me, so he couldn't teach you divine order. Some of you had father figures

but were so rebellious and disobedient, that you did what you wanted to do, no matter what your father told you. All that did not matter. I still took care of your every need, especially in your darkest hour. When I saw you thinking that you had failed in making right decisions, I, God, dispatched my messenger angels to bring you a rhema word in the night season to feed your spirit man, so that your natural man would be comforted. I opened doors for you that you did not walk through because you started looking at your own ability and your own strength. Know this: that I already made provision for you and went before you to make every crooked way straight. All I wanted was for you to take My yolk upon you and learn of Me, so that you would find rest unto your soul. You must begin to realize that it is My yolk that is easy and My burden that is light. I charge you now to go forth and be the man that I already ordained you to be, before you were formed in your mother's womb. I will always come and meet you where you are, so that you will not have to struggle trying to reach for me. I want you now, from this day forward, to cast your cares upon me for I, God, care for you. Everything you need is already in you. Tap into the treasures of life that were placed in you before the beginning, so that you can see the life that I intended for you. Take my hand and let me lead you from darkness into My marvelous light.

I have three sons and two grandsons. I want them to prosper and be the head of their families. I want God to cause them to walk in their priestly anointing as was God's intention in the beginning. God wants to cause His kingdom to manifest on this earth. He wants us to have territory over which we can rule and have dominion. He wants us to walk in peace with all men because He has given us peace that surpasses all understanding. He wants us to ask for wisdom so that we will walk with knowledge and understanding. In all our getting we must gain an understanding. Knowledge is power; however, knowledge without wisdom is dangerous. Without understanding, the knowledge that we have would cause us to operate in darkness. It would be like going through life blindfolded. Wisdom tells us when to move, with the knowledge we have. Understanding signals us to be still when what we know, tells us to move.

When a tree sheds its leaves it appears dead, however, it is usually going through a metamorphosis; with the coming of spring the trees grow new leaves. Squirrels help trees spread throughout the forest when they bury or store acorns for food.

Acorns, the nuts and seeds of oak trees, that are not dug up eventually take root and grow into new trees.

Jesus wants us to be a reproduction of Him so that we can have a fulfilling life. Before we do that we must know who Jesus is and why was He sent to the earth. The four gospels, Matthew, Mark, Luke, and John, recount Jesus' life while He was on the earth. Isaiah, the prophet, reveals the coming Messiah. When we need healing, we can know that God already healed us. In Isaiah 53:5 we find, *"But he was wounded for our transgressions, he was bruised for our iniquities: the chastisement of our peace was upon him; and with his stripes we are healed."* Since we were created to be a reproduction of Jesus, He made us more than conquerors. Some are gifted to heal people but they do not take the place of physicians because God also created them. Although, Jesus is the Great Physician, we were designed in His imagine after His likeness to walk in gifts of ministry He walked in. We have what Jesus has so therefore we must walk in the vocation for which we were called.

ISAIAH 53:5

Jesus fed five thousand with two loaves of bread and five fish. He took a small amount and multiplied it. We can do the same. I cooked dinner one evening and did not realize other people were coming over. However, I was able to stretch what I'd prepared so that we had more than enough; some took plates home. While I was preparing the food, I called on El Shaddai (A God who is more than enough).

We must plant in good soil, remove all the rocks, and get rid of bugs. In our lives we must be sure to get rid of those things that are not pleasing to the Lord so that we can sow on good ground. Sin is like weeds. Weeds take over and choke the life out of plants; sin does the same in our lives.

We must be careful how we conduct our lives because people learn more by example. God wants us to be productive. When we are strengthened, we must go back and strengthen the weak. Do not misunderstand me. If we abuse substance, God will not tell us to strengthen others in a similar situation. That's what the enemy wants. The 20/80 theory says that that the twenty bad will convert the eighty good. We must weigh the wisdom of a situation before we act. Old things must pass away behold they all should become new. New wine only goes into new wine skin.

Jesus wants us to produce the life of the Father economically, with order and responsibility. Economics means budgeting, saving, and purchasing goods to survive. First and foremost, we must pay our tithes and offerings to God; they belong to Him. We must sow our first fruit and offer it into God's kingdom. Paying our tithes and offerings bring order into our lives. We must also sow our money on good ground and examine our lifestyles. Anything that does not belong in our lives will defeat the purpose of giving. If we do not believe the law of giving, we will not receive an increase. Luke 6:38, "*Give, and it shall be given unto you; good measure, pressed down, and shaken together, and running over, shall men give unto your bosom. For with the same measure that ye mete withal it shall be measured to you again.*" Our blessings will overtake us. Blessings will run us down and almost knock us over. If we give, we will receive. Anticipate a return on our giving. We will reap whatever we sow. Giving opens the way for healing, protection, and wealth. It is part of our relationship with the Father that says, "I trust You to meet my every need." When we tithe, we tell God, "I trust You with 10 percent of my increase so that You can help me manage 90 percent." If someone gives us something, we should receive it graciously. Doing so will release the blessings to us and the giver.

MALACHI 3:10-12

Malachi 3:10-12 says, "*Bring ye all the tithes into the storehouse, that there may be meat in mine house, and prove me now herewith, saith the LORD of hosts, if I will not open you the windows of heaven, and pour you out a blessing, that there shall not be room enough to receive it. And I will rebuke the devourer for your sakes, and he shall not destroy the fruits of your ground; neither shall your vine cast her fruit before the time in the field, saith the LORD of hosts. And all nations shall call you blessed: for ye shall be a delightsome land, saith the LORD of hosts."*

Our cabinets will stay so full that we will have enough to always give to others. God wants to open the windows of Heaven and pour out a blessing that we will not have room enough to receive. We will lack no good thing.

Chapter Nine
The Fig Tree

(Mark 11:13)

"And seeing a fig tree afar off having leaves, he came, if haply he might find any thing thereon: and when he came to it, he found nothing but leaves; for the time of figs was not yet."

Once Adam and Eve realized they were naked they made clothing from the leaves of the fig tree; such a tree bears fruit and is therefore useful. A fig looks like a small pear but is brownish when ripe.

Jesus cursed a tree in Mark 11:13 because it bore no fruit; it was simply taking up space and absorbing nourishment. This should imply to the believers that we must continually produce fruit of the spirit. Galatians 5:22-23 says, *"But the fruit of the Spirit is love, joy, peace, longsuffering, kindness, goodness, faithfulness, meekness, self-control; against such things there is no law."* The flesh must be

MARK 11:13

GALATIANS 5:22-23

crucified of its passions and its lust. The flesh does its works without life; the Spirit brings forth fruit that is full of life.

During the time when Jesus entered Jerusalem, drove out those who defiled the temple, and ministered publicly He came to the fig tree and was ready to eat. When He saw that it was not producing figs, He cast it into the sea. Matthew the tax collector described what happened in Matthew 21:19-21. Mark 11:12-13 gives his account of the incident, also.

Fig trees were used as a sign that summer is approaching, in Matthew 24:32 says, "*Now learn a parable of the fig tree; When his branch is yet tender, and putteth forth leaves, ye know that summer is nigh*:"

Revelation 6:13 says, "*...a fig tree caseth her untimely figs, when she is shaken of a mighty wind.*" When the strong wind shakes the fig tree it produces premature figs. We must be sure to walk with God just like Enoch, who did not move ahead of God. God saw his works and caused Him not to see death. He was translated up to Heaven. (Genesis 5:24; Hebrews 11:5) We cannot move before it's time. When God gives us something, we cannot run with it until we hear Him say, "go." Stop moving ahead of yourself. Stay within the parameters of God but do not slack behind. When God is telling us to move, we must move.

We can learn a valuable lesson from the fig tree. If trees

MATTHEW 21:19-21

MARK 11:12-13

MATTHEW 24:32

REVELATION 6:13

GENESIS 5:24

HEBREWS 11:5

get too much or too little water and light, they become stressed. With us, if we do not drink enough water, eat the proper foods or get enough rest, we go through stress. Insects and diseases can affect the health of the tree. Some bugs eat the roots that are so important to a tree's health and damage the tree. If we are not rooted and grounded in the Word of God, life's struggles can destroy us. Beetles, fungi, viruses, and bacteria can attack the leaves and move from tree to tree shortening the lifespan of the affected trees. Some insects suck the sap of the tree, stopping the flow of the sap, which causes the tree to weaken. Chewing insects eat the tissue of the leaves. Sucking insects stick their beaks (proboscis) into the tissues of the leaves and branches. Boring insects are found beneath the bark. The adults lay eggs in tunnels beneath the bark while some, called bark beetles, mate at or near the surface of the bark.

We must be able to distinguish among the infectious diseases and other disorders to give the tree proper treatment. However, not all insects are destructive. Most are beneficial; some help with the pollination.

Joel 2:25 says, "*And I will restore to you the years that the locust hath eaten, the cankerworm, and the caterpiller, and the palmerworm, my great army which I sent among you.*" In our lives where the cankerworm and

JOEL 2:25

palmerworm came to devour, God will restore everything we thought we lost.

Thousands of pests go after trees, including:

- Bark beetle
- Blotch leaf miners
- Lace bug
- Leaf-chewing insects
- Mites
- Root-feeding white grub
- Scale insects
- Serpentine leaf miners
- Shoot moth larva
- Tent caterpillar egg mass
- Twig galls
- Twig Girdler
- Wood borer adult
- Wood borer larva

Knowing what insect is damaging the tree, will determine the treatment. When we cannot determine the problem, we will not be able to treat it properly. We may have to hire an arborist to deal with the problem. For more information on tree care go to www.treesaregood.com.

Jesus refers to us as trees. People who produce good fruit do the work of God. People who do not bring forth good fruit are cut off and cast out the same way Jesus cast out the fig tree. Luke 6:43 says, "*For a good tree bringeth not forth corrupt fruit; neither doth a corrupt tree bring forth good fruit.*" Matthew 7:17 says, "*Even so every good tree bringeth forth good fruit; but a corrupt tree bringeth forth evil fruit.*"

LUKE 6:43

MATTHEW 7:17

Chapter Ten
Olive Tree — The Anointing

(Nehemiah 5:11)

"Restore, I pray you, to them, even this day, their lands, their vineyards, their oliveyards, and their houses, also the hundredth part of the money, and of the corn, the wine, and the oil, that ye exact of them."

The Anointing destroys every yolk of bondage. Earlier, I talked about the different kinds of anointing and the hin of olive oil. Here I discuss the process involved to extract the oil from the olive.

An olive tree is a slow growing, crooked tree that was of immense value in biblical times. (Deuteronomy 6:11; Romans 11:17) The olive tree is a symbol of fruitfulness, and the branch of the olive tree is a symbol of peace. A cultivated tree grows to about twenty feet in height and can live several hundred

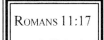

years. Oil from the tree's fruit has many uses.

Oil was an essential part of everyday life in biblical times (2 Kings 18:32; Matthew 25:3). It was used as medicine, for lamplight, in trade, religious ceremonies, food preparation, and cosmetics. Oil was used in the consecration of priests and kings. Among other things, oil symbolized joy (Isaiah 61:3; Psalms 45:7). Olive trees provide fruit for the valuable olive oil of the Middle East.

Nehemiah wanted the Lord to restore. Nehemiah is the last of the historical books called the minor prophets. Chapters 1-7, talk about Nehemiah's first governorship when he was the king's cupbearer. Nehemiah was more a man of action than of thoughts. Not only did he want the restoration, he let God use him to be a part of the work. His dependence was on God and not man.

While he was rebuilding the wall of Jerusalem, some questioned his work and authority not knowing he had already got permission from the king. When we get instructions from God to do something not everyone will agree with us. We must have a personal relationship with God so that we can hear clearly. We should obey God rather than man (Acts 5:29) He will not steer us wrong. He will even forewarn us of impending trouble.

2 KINGS 18:32
MATTHEW 25:3
ISAIAH 61:3
PSALMS 45:7
ACTS 5:29

The Olive Oil is Precious

When speaking about the anointing, I think of King David. (I Samuel 16:1-13) Samuel came over to Jesse's house because God instructed him to anoint one of Jesse's sons king over Israel. When he tried to pour the oil on David's brothers, the oil would not come out, so Samuel asked Jesse if he had any other sons. Jesse said yes, but he was out in the field tending the sheep and was dirty while the other sons were well groomed. When Samuel took the canister to pour the oil over David's head, it poured out, he was being prepared for great things but he had to go through a rigorous learning process before he became king over Israel.

I SAMUEL 16:1-13

First Chronicles 27:28 says, "*And over the olive trees and the sycamore trees that were in the low plains was Bealhanan the Gederite: and over the cellars of oil was Joash.*" The olive trees and sycamore trees were so important that they and the cellars where the oil was stored were guarded. King David did not just select any men to protect the olive trees and the cellars of oil. He made sure he picked the strongest and greatest men.

I CHRONICLES 27:28

In midwinter, after the olives become black on the trees, they are harvested either by hand or with mechanical shakers.

The olives are ground into a paste to release the oil droplets from flesh. The oil and water in the paste are extracted by powerful hydraulic presses. The oil-water mixture is pumped into large settling tanks, where the lighter oil rises to the top and is drawn off. This oil is mixed with warm water and then separated by a machine, using centrifugal force for separating substances of different densities, for removing moisture, or for simulating gravitational effects. This final step may be repeated several times to remove bitterness from the oil.

We can use olive oil to anoint our homes. We must first pray that God gives us insight about what to do and what to say while anointing our homes. I do this any time I purchase a new home or move into a new apartment, and even after time goes by. I also do this while traveling in a different car, in a new office, arriving at hotels, during trips or handling any new equipment, etc. I anoint the doors, doorknobs, walls, windows and any other area or person in the house that the Lord leads me to anoint. Listen to the instructions from the Lord. He tells us when it is time.

I ask that the blood of Jesus cover and surround my home to protect me from any hurt, harm, or danger. I can speak life into my home by speaking positively about myself and everyone else in my home. I ask God to dispatch Michael, the head of the warring angels, to come and fight for me while anointing my home. I remind God that His Word says, *"That you have given us power over serpents and scorpions and over all the works of the enemy and none will hurt us."*

We need to destroy everything evil in the house and replace it with the presence of God. God inhabits the praises of His people. Sing a love song unto the Lord and sing praises to Him. Command that every foul spirit and anything that is not like God be removed and cast into the sea (lake of fire) that burns forever.

We need to remove anything that is not pleasing in God's sight. We need to ask Him to show us, so that we will know, and then get a trash bag in which to throw it out. Repeat over and over, "For the weapons of our warfare are not carnal but they are mighty through God to the pulling down of strongholds and bringing into captivity every thought to the obedience of Christ." Remind God that His Word says that, "No weapon formed against you [and yours] shall prosper and every tongue that would rise up against you in judgment shall be condemned."

ROMANS 8:28

We can pray that His will be done on earth even as it is in heaven. Quote Romans 8:28, *"... all things work together for the good of them who love the Lord and who are the called according to His purpose."* Say, "When the enemy comes in, like a flood the spirit of the Lord will raise a standard against him." Repeat, "When the enemy comes in one way, he must flee seven ways."

Say the entire 91st no. of Psalms aloud:

PSALMS 91

"*He that dwelleth in the secret place of the most High shall abide under the shadow of the Almighty. I will say of the LORD, He is my refuge and my fortress: my God; in him will I trust. Surely he shall deliver thee from the snare of the fowler, and from the noisome pestilence. He shall cover thee with his feathers, and under his wings shalt thou trust: his truth shall be thy shield and buckler. Thou shalt not be afraid for the terror by night; nor for the arrow that flieth by day; Nor for the pestilence that walketh in darkness; nor for the destruction that wasteth at noonday. A thousand shall fall at thy side, and ten thousand at thy right hand; but it shall not come nigh thee. Only with thine eyes shalt thou behold and see the reward of the wicked. Because thou hast made the LORD, which is my refuge, even the most High, thy habitation; There shall no evil befall thee, neither shall any plague come nigh thy dwelling. For he shall give his angels charge over thee, to keep thee in all thy ways. They shall bear thee up in their hands, lest thou dash thy foot against a stone. Thou shalt tread upon the lion and adder: the young lion and the dragon shalt thou trample under feet. Because he hath set his love upon me, therefore will I deliver him:*

I will set him on high, because he hath known my name.
He shall call upon me, and I will answer him: I will be
with him in trouble; I will deliver him, and honour him.
With long life will I satisfy him, and shew him my
salvation."

Walk with an assurance that God can do anything but fail.
While we anoint our homes, we must believe that God is a
rewarder of them that diligently seek Him.

Chapter Eleven
Family Tree — The Order

The proper order is God, Jesus, Holy Spirit, husband, wife, and then the children. Today many families are broken. The father is no longer with the family or the mother does not want to have anything to do with her husband or the children. Some children do not know their identity so they are going around like a city with no walls. Anything can come in and go out.

Ideally the father would teach the children different trades while mothers would teach the children skills. It is God's desire that we keep order because He is a God of order. He has always been for the family. He created the family before He created the church. A spouse who does not want to stay and keep the family together should be allowed to go. We should not hold on to anyone that does not want to stay with us. Life goes on and it does not stop at one person. God will be a father for the fatherless and a mother for the motherless. He will keep our minds in perfect peace when our minds are stayed on Him. In this 21st Century, roles have really changed for the father and mother. Most husbands and wives are both working long hours and the household still needs to be well kept.

A Revelation of a Family

A family is a corporation run by the CEO (the father), that consults our Heavenly Father before making decisions. Because of Jesus Christ the father can go directly to God and get consultation from Him to establish and organize God's plan and purpose for his family. The second in command is the mother; she delegates chores to the children the family employees. Some parents own their own businesses while others work to make others rich.

The father and mother work for companies known as clients that pays the parents a salary for their services. The parents use the money to manage their household, something that is not as easy as it seems. Bills must be paid on time, the house must be cleansed daily, the lawn must be mowed and watered, the laundry must be done, food and other necessities must be purchased and stored properly in order to run the household conveniently.

The father delegates tasks to the mother to keep the home

running smoothly. The mother delegates tasks to the children. Fathers who do not travel and spend time at home are able to give the children instructions while the mother makes sure the tasks are done correctly. Everybody has a role in running the household. Roles have changed from how it was done years ago.

Parents invest in the children to maintain the household. When we invest in something we expect a return. If we spend money and time with our children we anticipate a return on our investment. I told my children, "If I spend X amount of dollars to send you to school, in return I expect you to finish, become successful, become independent and pass what I taught YOU on to the next generation."

Some investments are long-term while others are short-term. The latter are riskier. In long-term investments we can lose money along the way but gain a lot in the end. When we invest in stock, we take the risk of losing everything. Smart investors diversify rather than investing everything in one kind of stock, bond, money market, annuity or other investment form. They also insure their lives so that if anything happens to them, the family will be covered. We need to seek God's advice when it comes to our money so that we might become good stewards over our money. Money answers all things (Ecclesiastes 10:19).

ECCLESIASTES
10:19

If the father is out of position, the mother steps in and handles the business of the family. It is not an easy task. Whoever manages the family corporation should consult God on a daily basis on what to do next. He will cause His kingdom to come on the earth as it is in heaven. There are administrators, economists, and so many others in heaven. Remember God sits high on the thrown, looks low and He looks beyond our faults and see to our every need.

There is power in unity. Have family gatherings and functions at least four times a year one at least once a year if the family is spread out. This way we see what spirits are in the family and know what we need to pray.

The Sap of a Tree

Sap is the thin, watery fluid inside plants that circulates food and water to the different parts of the plant. Maple syrup is the concentrated sap obtained from maple and black maple. Sap flows intermittently for periods of up to six weeks, is caught in buckets, strained, and concentrated by boiling to a density for syrup or evaporated further for sugar.

The sap of the rubber tree is used to make latex, which is vulcanized to make rubber. Other non-tree plants also have sap, such as euphorbias (including poinsettias) and milkweeds, although the word sap is commonly only used to refer to trees.

Most Pará rubber is produced of the family Euphorbiaceae (spurge family), which is produced from trees grown on plantations in Asia and to a lesser extent in Africa. The tree is tapped by making careful incisions. Once the trees are five to six years old, they can be tapped at approximately thirty degrees. Tapping at the right angle and at the right time will not stunt the tree's growth.

Some of us are waiting on God to position us and give us a mantle to carry. However, God knows that if He put us in a certain place too soon, it will stunt our growth. I find the Lord using me a little here and a little there to see how I will handle situations.

Souls are at stake, and He does not want to have people in positions that would not consider the price Jesus paid for that soul. He wants us to be fully equipped and ready for ministry. This is to ensure that we do not abort or miscarry His plan and purpose when faced with adversities.

Maple trees are found mainly in temperate regions and on tropical mountain slopes. Some maple trees are used for cabinets or furniture. The close-grained varieties are used for shipbuilding and aircraft construction and floors; the scraps left from these are used for fuel.

We must be in a state of pleasantness, walking in self-control and calmness especially when our environment is hostile and chaotic. While we are in a state of confusion, God cannot use us because we are not able to think clearly. Just as the maple tree grows in a temperate region, we grow better and deal with situations better when things around us are peaceful. Unfortunately that is not always the case. I have learned to pull on God's peace by taking deep breathes, keeping my mind stayed on Him and bringing my thoughts captive to the obedience of Christ when situations tempt me to react, with hostility. When I react hastily, I regret the things I say. When we regret actions or words that come from haste, we need to pray and let the fruit of the Spirit take over from now on.

Traditions

A tradition is a practice or a belief that creates positive feelings; it is handed down from one generation to another. Deuteronomy 4:9-10 says, *"Only take heed to thyself, and keep thy soul diligently, lest thou forget the things which thine eyes have seen, and lest they depart from thy heart all the days of thy life: but teach them thy sons, and thy sons' sons; Specially the day that thou stoodest before the LORD thy God in Horeb, when the LORD said unto me, Gather me the people together, and I will make them hear my words, that they may learn to fear me all the days that they shall live upon the earth, and that they*

DEUTERONOMY 4:9-10

may teach their children."

A family must get together and flow together, the way sap flows through various parts of the tree, to produce something that can be reproduced over and over again and is beneficial to the family. Remember fruit does not fall far from the tree. Dysfunctions in a family stop the flow. When we allow our flesh to make decisions for us, we deny our spirit man's control over our situations. There are two natures beneath our breast: one we love, the other we hate; whichever one we feed will dominate.

If we continue to do the works of the flesh, we will reap those works. Everything that we do in the natural has spiritual repercussion. Some family men and/or women start a business and pass it on to their sons/daughters who are grateful to continue the tradition. Some parents would like for their children to follow in their footsteps but the children decided to do something else. Some children become very successful while others don't. Neither is better than the other. Whatever a person decides, he or she must develop a personal relationship with the Father. This concept should be passed on from generation to generation.

Families have remedies that work and some that don't. Our mothers may have used a favorite remedy of their grandmothers to make us feel better when we got sick. Some wives tales and fables sound pretty foolish. Such as if you put your purse on the floor, you will never have any money. This is foolishness. A good steward over money will always have more than enough.

Families pass recipes down from generation to generation; some meals are tied to specific holidays. Although we have family remedies and recipes, we should not be afraid to try something new. We must allow Holy Spirit to guide and lead us into new ideas and new avenues and be prepared to change as the Spirit leads.

People of God should not want to be lucky because luck comes and goes. They should want God's blessings to flow in their lives all the time, not periodically. If we keep doing the same thing expecting different results, we are likely to be disappointed. We must stop going around with the same mindset believing that the same thing over and over again will have different results.

We must keep moving forward. If we do not press on and continue we might find ourselves going in circles. The Lord recently told me that I must not be afraid of the blessings that He wants to shower upon me. Every time I was at the brink of a breakthrough, I found myself going back to what I was more familiar with again and again, even though it had not worked. I had created a comfort zone and stayed there instead of pressing ahead into new and spirit-led grounds. I found myself putting trust in men and things. God wants to be my source. He wants me to trust in Him wholeheartedly. He wants me to get in His vein and follow Him so that He can take me higher (precept upon percept; line upon line; here a little there a little). He wants His glory to rest upon my shoulders.

God made a promise to Abraham and his seed. We are Abraham's seed. In Genesis 22:17-18 God says, "*That in blessing I will bless thee, and in multiplying I will multiply thy seed as the stars of the heaven, and as the sand which is upon the sea shore; and thy seed shall possess the gate of his enemies; And in thy seed shall all the nations of the earth be blessed; because thou hast obeyed my voice.*"

> GENESIS
> 22:17-18

Abraham listened to the voice of God when the Lord told him to sacrifice his son Isaac. When Abraham was about to slay Isaac with a knife, a ram appeared in the bush. He heard an angel of the Lord calling Him. Because Abraham was obedient, God blessed him and his seed. It is confirmed in Galatians 3:29 which says, "*And if ye be Christ's, then are ye Abraham's seed, and heirs according to the promise.*" We must know without a doubt that we are heirs to the throne. God made that provision for us at creation.

> GALATIANS 3:29

Heirlooms

A family heirloom is passed from one generation to the next; it can be big or small; it can have monetary or sentimental value.

An inheritance is a legacy. We received the blessings of the Lord from Abraham. We received an incorruptible inheritance through Jesus Christ. Acts 26:18 says, *"To open their eyes, and to turn them from darkness to light, and from the power of Satan unto God, that they may receive forgiveness of sins, and inheritance among them which are sanctified by faith that is in me."* The legacy that the Lord left us is the blessings of the promised land that He gave to Abraham, Isaac, and Jacob; the land that flows with milk and honey. Milk represents our needs being met, and honey represents our desires being met. Everything we need has been placed inside of us.

In order to stirrup our spirit men and women we must spend time studying God's word, devote time for prayer, and spend time in His presence (praise and worship). We must mingle with Christians who have a heart toward God and who are sold out for Him. Iron sharpens iron; therefore, we must be with others who spend time feeding their spirit man and

ACTS 26:18

spirit woman. We are already born into iniquity so doing things in the flesh comes natural. When our spirit men and women tap into our intellect, we will operate in the things of God naturally most of the time. It will become apart of our everyday lives.

Our minds and thoughts will either move us closer or farther away from God. In the past we may have blamed God for things. We started looking at God in a negative way because bad things happened to us. Just because we decide to have a personal relationship with the Father does not mean we will not go through difficult times. When we are faced with adversity, we start losing faith and stop believing. We turn away from Him and do not want to have anything to do with anyone who speaks about how good He is. This is one of the tricks of the enemy. When we give the enemy full range over our lives things get worse and we are afraid to return back to God.

Because of Jesus Christ death and resurrection, we have a right to return to the Father. God is always waiting with open arms to receive us. He wants only the best for us. He is waiting to welcome us back. Matthew 11: 28-30, "*Come unto me, all ye that labour and are heavy laden, and I will give you rest. Take my yoke upon you, and learn of me; for I am meek and lowly in heart: and ye shall find rest unto your souls. For my yoke is easy, and my burden is light.*"

MATTHEW
11:28-30

Healing Sap

In Jeremiah Chapter 8 the children of Israel had backslidden and started worshipping idol gods. They would not repent and continued living their lives in vain. They rejected the word of the Lord and the wisdom in it. The prophets and the priest dealt falsely. They healed the daughters slightly saying peace, peace; when there was no peace. God was hurt because of the hurt of His daughters. Jeremiah asked a question in 8:22, *"...is there no balm in Gilead; is their no physician there."* Then he asked about the health of the daughters.

Jeremiah 8:22

The balm Jeremiah was referring to was the healing sap from God. When mothers are wounded and hurting, they function and operate from a wounded spirit. They walk in bondage and not with liberty. The nurturing and proper training that they should give to the children are replaced with the things of this world. Once they decide to turn to the Lord for deliverance and strength, they cause the balm in Gilead to heal them. The healing sap flows throughout their bodies bringing to life the things that were lying dormant.

When everyone in the family is healthy, they can focus more on building the family spiritually, economically, and physically. Family members must get together and decide to become corporations and open family franchises. God wants us to own territory that we can pass on to the next generation. He did not put us together to sit around and create disasters and dysfunctions. He made us to rule and have dominion on the earth. He created us to have authority. This is why when we work to build someone else's business, we feel out of place. We were designed to have our own businesses. We need to take a moment and even move to seek the face of God over our businesses and what He would have us do, today. He would make a way and surely see us triumph.

The Cycle Starts Again

When the tree starts growing leaves again, the leaves come back larger and fuller. When it seems as if we have lost everything and that all hope is gone we must not give up. What looked lost will be found. What was old will become new. We begin to look better and feel better about life. We start blossoming into a lovely garden that spreads wide and grows tall. Just like Christ dying on the cross for us; when Mary Magdalene thought He was gone, an angel came to tell her, "He has risen." He rose and gave us life and gave it to us that more abundantly. He came to redeem us back to God. We had fallen into sin but God had a plan. His plan was to make things right; the way He intended life to be for us. He only wants the best for us. We must stop settling for mediocrity.

The blood of the Lamb paid the price to make us alive again; to bring us back to the place where the Father wanted us to be.

If we look at circumstances in life and they seem dead, we should not believe that they will not come back stronger and better. Things must die in order for new things to surface. The third day will come about when that which seemed dead comes alive. The third day is important because what seemed dead was only planted. When seeds are planted they go through the process of vegetation. The seeds start growing under the ground before they surface. Once they surface we see the buds and the breaking of a new day.

Old things must pass away and behold all things become new. This time, when we start growing we are careful of what we allow in our space. We remember what happened to get us to a point of dying. Dying to self is not all that bad. But we must be broken and change must take place. If we are determined to allow a metamorphosis to take place in our lives, we will come back with a power from on high. What God predestine will manifest. It is already done. We will walk in such a way that people will wonder what is going on in our lives. We will look a lot different.

Struggles are good because they teach us what to do the next time around. This time we cannot give up on Christ; we must hold God's unchanging hands.

Now is the time to give our lives to Christ. We will never be perfect until the day of Jesus Christ, so we must stop looking at our righteousness, because it is as a filthy rag in His sight. God sees us as if we did not sin. He looks at us through the blood of Jesus Christ. Because Jesus died for our sins, we have a right to the tree of life. His suffering redeemed us back to the Father. When He was beaten furiously, nailed to the cross (tree), and resurrected, the earth quaked, the dead got up and walked, and the veil was ripped in two. He took the sting out of death for us. He rose with all power in His hands, and that is where we reside. No man can pluck us out.

Jesus left His glory to come to this sinful world, to suffer and die so that by His resurrection we too will never die in our sin but live forever with Him. We must not let His death on the cross for us be in vain. We must reach out to Him today. He is waiting to receive us and give us a new robe of hope, our peace and more.

Jesus is our propitiator. Jesus was the Lamb that was sacrificed for our sins. Now we have divine forgiveness and favor with God. Because of Jesus, God's mercy and grace is extended to us and puts us back in a right relationship with the Father. We receive new mercy every morning and His grace is sufficient to keep us to the ends of the world.

To know who we are in Him we must repeat this Pledge:

By the authority and power invested in me. By the Biblical truths and laws govern by Heaven. Based on the Blood of the Lamb that was shed for my sins. I have been officially ordained as one of God's ambassadors. Standing on Isaiah 54:17, that states no weapon that is formed against me shall be able to prosper.

ISAIAH 54:17

I agree with Paul when he taught in Romans 10:9 that if I would confess with my mouth the Lord Jesus and believe in my heart that God has raised Jesus from the dead that I am saved. My lifestyle will exemplify the power of the resurrection. I am in constant consultation with Jesus Christ through the Holy Spirit for the purposes set forth in whatever I put my hands to do will prosper.

ROMANS 10:9

According to every Executive Order, I will be steadfast unmovable always abiding in the things of God. This order cannot be changed, overwritten, vetoed or diverted because of past, present and future circumstances. I will keep this and all future prayers in mind when faced with adversities.

This is my word of honor.

Trees

Fig trees

    Apple trees

        Olive trees

            Cedar trees

                Oak trees

Adam and Eve knew the value of a tree.
No longer will they enjoy paradise with its many
splendor trees.
Oh! But, it is too late.
You two gave up the garden over one tree.

Let us consider for a moment:
What would life be without a tree?

Well, there will be no recordings of a family tree.
How would we handle our financial tree?
What would you use to grow our fruit tree?
Where would a carpenter obtain his trade's material tree
especially when the foundation of a home is the tree.

By: *Valerie Gilmer*

A lifelong Chicago resident, **Minister Kathy McClure** has been a legal secretary in Illinois for over seventeen years. She has her ministerial license and was ordained to preach and teach the gospel in October 1992 at Greater Mount Caramel M.B. Church where she had been a member since 1985, and taught Sunday school to seasoned women every Sunday for three years. This mother of five and grandmother of three is currently working on her next book while taking extended classes at Valley Kingdom Ministries International ("VKMI") where she has been a member for over five years. Throughout the year, she prepares meals for homeless shelters under the umbrella of Shama Ministries.

Min. McClure's nationwide tour begins Spring 2007 and she will present seminars and lectures how to succeed in life. Her vision is to see people give their lives to Christ so that they can live a full productive life of success and prosperity. Life will bring struggles that are unimaginable. It takes a genius to look at a problem and see it as an opportunity to succeed™. Before you get to a point of giving up, reach up and grab hold of the promises of God, which is Yea and Amen. (II Corinthians 1:20)

God gave her I Corinthians 9:16 to stand on ("*For though I preach the gospel, I have nothing to glory of: for necessity is laid upon me; yea, woe is unto me, if I preach not the gospel.*").

CPSIA information can be obtained at www.ICGtesting.com
Printed in the USA
LVOW08s1310211013

357813LV00002B/71/A